Responses

★★★★ *"Johnson steps outside a rigid psychological format and offers a refreshing humorous and radically honest approach that immediately puts the reader at ease. This book deserves to be and should be available in every school and public library."*
-Rita Hanly
MEDITATION MAGAZINE

★★★★ *"CREATIVE REBELLION is an ever-flowing spring of truth, wisdom and spirit-centered love. I've given it to my teenage son with my blessing, and, in reading it myself, was truly inspired and enlightened. This is the best book I have ever found for young adults (and their parents). It's a godsend!"*
-Carol Kramer
BODY MIND SPIRIT MAGAZINE

★★★★ *"CREATIVE REBELLION talks to teens, to those who live and work with teens, and the message has that special grace of illumination. He writes with joy, he thinks differently, his counseling is gentle.Very simple ways to discover yourself."*
-Jay Bail
THE BOOK READER

★★★★ *"Reading CREATIVE REBELLION gave me new ideas about how I can take over my body and mind so I can have better control over my own life."*
-Teresa, Age 17
Pueblo, CO

★★★★ *"Very enlightening, written not only for teenagers, but for all people who enjoy life to its fullest."*
-Jim, Father of teenagers
Grand Junction, CO

★★★★ *"This book will definitely shake your thoughts. CREATIVE REBELLION is extremely meaningful and inspiring to the true rebel."*
-Valerie, Age 15
Bainbridge Island, WA

★★★★ *"I like the casual style, as if you are sitting, talking to a friend."*
-Brian Enright
COMMUNITY RESOURCE PUBLICATIONS
Los Angeles, CA

★★★★ *"Comprehensive and timely, with some very good ideas."*
-STEPPING STONE LITERARY AGENCY

OTHER BOOKS BY
DANIEL (SHAHID) JOHNSON

YHANTISHOR: A FANTASY BASED IN TRUTH

*YHANTISHOR: UND DIE GLASPERLEN IM
DSCHUNGEL* (German Translation)

FORTHCOMING: NON-FICTION

HOW TO REACH REBELLIOUS TEENAGERS

FICTION

THE AZTEC CAVE OF LIFE

THE TAKING OF NANIN

CREATIVE
Rebellion

POSITIVE OPTIONS FOR TEENS IN THE 90s

Written and Illustrated
by

Daniel S. Johnson

Mystic Garden Press
Crestone, CO

CREATIVE REBELLION
POSITIVE OPTIONS FOR TEENS IN THE 90s

Written and Illustrated By
DANIEL S. JOHNSON

Published by

 Mystic Garden Press
BOX 51, CRESTONE, CO 81131-0051 U.S.A.

The author gratefully acknowledges the aid of Ilse Johnson for editing, Roy Gould, Amrit Hanrahan and Bhagwato Pennick for cover art, Crystal Dickerson, Talmath and Nakia Dennett as models, Karin DiGiacomo and The Manitou Foundation for technical and moral support, Marge Whitlock of SLV Secretarial Service, Rebekah Sowards of the Adams State College print shop and Ye Olde Print Shoppe of Alamosa for technical assistance, and much thanks to Mati Johnson for putting up with this whole mess.

Library of Congress Catalog Card Number   91-061346

ISBN 0-922848-11-4

Fully Indexed

 Printed in the United States of America
on acid-free, recycled paper

CONTENTS

Dedicated Gratefully To
OSHO
Whose Love and Insights
Inspired This Book

and
To TEENAGERS Everywhere

FOREWORD

Another book for teenagers? Wait! The framework of CREATIVE REBELLION is entirely different from other books for teens. A book for teenagers should be written by someone like Daniel, who can so easily access his inner child with a spontaneity which most adults seem to have forgotten or chosen to discard. Over the last twenty years, I've worked in a variety of adolescent programs. With the best of intentions, the usual modality of treatment in these centers has been behavior modification. Within this rigid system, we sometimes forget the human element and why we are here in the first place. CREATIVE REBELLION reminds us.

Given the number of teens who participate in these treatment programs, I can't imagine a better text to use and I highly recommend it to other professionals in adolescent psychiatric units. When teens are in trouble, there is a great seriousness which surrounds them and levity is needed, lightness and humor are extremely healing. This is not just another self-help book for teens, but a book to introduce options, knowing all have to make it on their own.

Teenagers often feel that they are doomed to depression and may need to be reminded that it's okay to experience the joy and spontaneity which is their inherent birthright. Adult pressure to grow up need not squelch their happiness. Parents should be guides and friends, not owners and loyalties must not be misplaced on abusive parents.

This book provides the fortification and the permission for teens to evolve to their unique potentials, instead of accepting false limitations. It is vitally important for our children to know that there is help for them when they need it.

I would like to see this evolve into a teenage underground where participants can share insights and stop hiding human emotions. Give a man a fish and you've fed him dinner, teach a man to fish and you feed him for a lifetime. Personal transformation can be integrated into our daily lives but it takes a snap of reality, an invitation to personal experience, a delightfully shocking book called CREATIVE REBELLION!

Adolescent Therapist   Anya Dolan
St. Vincent Hospital
Santa Fe, NM, 1991

PREFACE

Are you a rebel? A misfit? Do you sometimes suspect or hope that you are just visiting this planet? Are you bored or angry with this time of your life? Does everything you do that's fun get you in trouble? If so, this book was written for you. If not, please close the cover and return to your herd.

In the past, teens were "kept in line" with force; punishment was the accepted means for controlling behavior. During the eighties, force was met with violence, suicide, drug abuse and extreme isolation. What has changed? One reason is that you are more intelligent and more informed on current events than previous teens.

What about love? Sex is certainly running near the top of the popularity poll, but love and compassion seem to have become totally uncool. Why, with effective birth control methods widely available is the occurrence of AIDS and teen pregnancy rising?

Who cares? Has everyone degenerated into machines, with no feelings? The society seems more interested in efficiency and competition than in basic human emotions. But, who says you have to join them? Check it out, do business people look happy? What about those who don't succeed and wind up on the streets?

More than ever, GANGS are forming which are based in drugs, theft and violence. Prisons are filled with teenagers, mostly Black and Hispanic, where they learn to become professional criminals. People are afraid to be alone.

DRUGS are everywhere, and they are not all "soft" drugs which were used widely in the 60s for self-searching. Crack and ice, smack and crank are all horribly dangerous and easy to purchase. But drugs in themselves are not the problem, no matter what politicians say in trying to be popular. The real problem is the rampant ANGUISH of today's youth which makes drugs attractive as a means of escape or entertainment.

Why are most teens unhappy? Is there a way to become blissful and fun-loving again? Absolutely! This book will examine the roots of anguish, offer some methods of healing, will shock, tickle and kindle a fire in you, challenging you to reach to your highest potential with no preaching or teaching ...only reaching.

People are not allowed to live naturally, to go the direction their hearts yearn to go. In protest, teens are dropping out of school, listening to violent Heavy Metal music or dressing like corpses to snub the "too serious" society. But, is this FREEDOM?

Are you rebellious enough to follow your HEART instead of being manipulated by destructive peer pressure? I have no intentions of shoving you back into the society if you don't want to be there. Neither am I trying to stir up a revolution.

The 90s may be our last chance to choose life or death on this wonderful planet. With all the energies of youth, you can make the difference and turn around this vicious cycle of exploiting our environment, but first, you have to be joyous and celebrative yourself. Otherwise, what do you have to share? Past generations are handing you an abused Earth which they screwed up in the name of personal wealth. Are you going to accept this way of life and finish killing it?

The 90s have brought upon teens more problems than ever before, but also more OPPORTUNITIES. As helpless as each of us feels, we CAN make a difference! I'm introducing ways to remove anger and emotional pain, freeing your energies for love and creativity. Only a conscious person can find new and positive ways to deal with pollution, radiation, the ozone layer, poverty, famine and over-population. Hey, dudes, let's get ON it!

The joy of living, with inner integrity, can return with the introduction of POSITIVE INDIVIDUALITY. To step out of the insanity of the past will take much experience, insight and guts. First you have to know yourself, touching the source of life within, finding the truth no matter how painful it is to drop the consoling lies you've been taught to believe.

Because the focus of this book is on individual experimentation, it is as relevant for teens living in big cities as it is for those in small towns, as powerful for blacks, whites, reds, yellows and purples. My TEENWORK workshops are spontaneous and always changing as is life itself. These workshops only include teenagers who are personally interested in the science of knowing themselves and no one should be FORCED to join, or to read this book.

Truth is not a commodity which can be bought, sold or given to another. Truth can only be based in personal experience and, once you have experienced truth, it is yours. There are ways to aid individuals to attain to pure experiences of awareness and these are what I offer. No guarantees, it's up to you.

So, if you're ready to explore the unknown depths of your own consciousness: drop that skateboard, put away the makeup and take a step into the world of CREATIVE REBELLION. You just might meet YOURSELF.

AUTHOR'S NOTE: This is not a sexist book. I love and support all CREATIVE REBELS, male and female. Unfortunately, it was driving me bananas to write he/she, his/hers every time so I'm alternating gender whenever I feel like it.

CHAPTER ONE

REBELLION
OR REVOLUTION

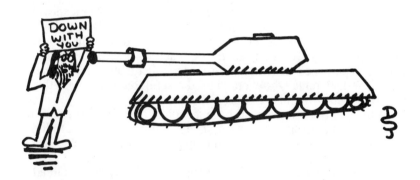

REBELLION is not merely another name for revolution. Consider that revolution comes from the same root as "revolve". Revolution is cyclic, eventually coming back to where it started, and back to the original problem.

Politically, revolution takes a stand against the established society and its rules so a new set of rules can be substituted. The Russian Revolution illustrates the usual outcome of violence. The revolutionaries became as horrible, if not worse than the Czar they overthrew, leading to seventy years of repression and terror.

REBELLION, by my definition, is not AGAINST anything, but FOR yourself. A dictionary definition includes "opposing any control". A true rebel must act out of his own inner feelings and intelligence, rather than blindly following orders.

The hard part here is that we've all been so conditioned into beliefs that it is difficult to differentiate between our true feelings, and what we've been taught to think, feel and respond to, most of which is absurd. Our given beliefs depend on where we are born, not on what is true.

Children don't come with instructions and most parents have no training, except the memories of how they were treated by their parents. Each generation passes on its ideas of morality and proper behavior to the next generation, compounding the gift with their own ideas. Whether a child is considered good or bad depends on how willing they are to obey the mountains of enforced behavioral expectations handed to them.

Do you remember reading in school about the Constitution and all the FREEDOMS you'll be allowed when you grow up? What child is allowed even Freedom of Speech? Do you feel respected as a human being without having to earn it? There is usually only one way to be accepted and that is to obey whatever your parents, teachers, churches and other adults demand of you.

Don't misunderstand the intentions. All these people mean well and a certain amount of discipline is needed so kids won't play in the highway, eat only chocolate and burn down the house. Punishment may well be needed as a teaching device, but often a child gets punished without a clear reason other than he has thought for himself. Parents who were abused as children often vent their anger on their own kids.

Whatever the issue, we all have a choice: do I OBEY or not? If not, is it worth the punishment? Also, as a teenager you have to look behind your instinct to refuse--is it to my benefit and am I intelligent enough to say YES when it is?

Imagine for a moment that you are a parent. (Maybe you already are.) Can you imagine the patience it takes to feed, clothe, supply housing and put up with all the antics, questions and foolishness of kids? Intelligent kids are the worst as they are always exploring, tinkering with everything and bombarding parents with unanswerable questions. If you supply an answer, it isn't enough, they want to have their own experiences, make their own mistakes and be independent.

Most parents choose to stifle intelligent children by instilling fear or creating guilt. Bribery is accepted also. "Be good or Santa won't bring you anything for Christmas!" "You can't do that because you'll fail, it's dangerous."

Parents want to protect their children and hope to prevent their kids from having to learn the hard way, as they did. Still, there is only one way to learn most things: direct experience. That doesn't mean you stupidly step in front of a car to see if you'll be killed.

So much information has been poured into our little heads that we think we know things that are unknowable. For example, religions grab tiny babies and induct them into the churches, possibly twenty years before the child might become interested in spirituality. By instilling wild beliefs in a small child, the very quest for truth is thwarted and the child learns to parrot ideas with no understanding of what he is saying. All he knows is that he is accepted by his parents and community by repeating these ideas.

Of course, a baby cannot be rebellious. She is so dependent on her parents that she learns quickly how to manipulate situations. Watch a new mother and her child and you can see the beginnings of politics. (Polite and politic come from the same root.) The baby learns that smiling brings positive attention, while a loud scream creates concern.

Power games develop between the generations. Certainly, the mother can WIN any argument because she has years of experience, is more articulate and is many times bigger. A mother knows that her absence can be traumatic and I've heard some mothers threaten to leave if the child doesn't obey. This creates an even bigger dependence which may influence all relationships in the future.

Children are very limited in physical power but come equipped with an incredible potential for making trouble. The earliest form of getting attention is an inescapable set of vocal chords, equalled only by air horns on semi-trucks. Given time, the scream will evolve into a cry for independence, a demand for equality: the everpresent rejection, "NO!"

Come on, admit it, doesn't saying NO give you a feeling of power? No? As two-year-olds, we never see that repeating NO all the time limits our freedom. The question is, do we ever outgrow the pseudo-power of negativity?

The revolutionary is one who is stuck in "NO". Whatever the promises, revolution is negative, a driving force to beat the chosen enemy in the name of freedom or justice. Revolution is always bound to fail because its methodology is negative. To be victorious, one has to become just like the enemy.

REBELLION has a totally different flavor. The rebel moves in the direction her heart and intelligence lead. She cannot be swayed by public opinion, peer pressure or other judgments. Rebels can listen to others without prejudice before deciding which avenue sounds best, but it is ultimately her decision.

Does this sound SELFISH? It is. If you are not selfish, you will never have enough joy to share with others. How can you give what you don't have? Once you love yourself and nurture your needs, a miracle happens: you become so overflowing with joy that you naturally share it with whomever you meet.

All societies teach members not to be selfish. You must serve others, SACRIFICE yourself for the next generation. But the next generation will be told also to sacrifice, so who ever gets to enjoy? I was always told to give the largest piece of cake to the other. What I learned was that I didn't deserve the best, and learned to be polite instead of authentic.

Selfishness is natural. Imagine a baby crying because someone else is hungry. He'll starve. He has to make it clear, "I am hungry ... NOW!" Notice how animals take their food away from the crowd to eat if they can.

In our society, being natural causes GUILT. If you are selfish, angry, weak or scared, sexual or passionate, you are considered an animal. Makes you want to growl, doesn't it? All the religions of the past have used guilt to condemn humanity and keep us in misery.

As a rebel, life is allowed to flow naturally, without interfering. This is not to say that you can never say NO. Sometimes you have to say YES to your NO also. This is true freedom. With freedom comes RESPONSIBILITY.

Just the mention of the word responsibility and thousands of teenage ears close automatically. Why? It's because the word has been perverted to mean DUTY (which is a four-letter word). An adult often uses the word responsibility to mean, "You are not acting responsible unless you do exactly what I tell you to do." This is blackmail.

The actual meaning of responsibility is THE ABILITY TO RESPOND. Simple, eh? Remember that RESPONSE is not reaction. Reaction is always unconscious, mechanical. Someone hits you and you return the insult. Response is conscious. Despite what has been done to you, you remain intelligent and decide what course is right for you.

If you REACT, the other is the boss. You are not free if you can be pushed into a fight. RESPONSE is spontaneous. You remain the master of yourself. With response, you'll never have to look back and say, "I'm sorry, I didn't mean to do that." You choose what to do and you mean it.

Now, this doesn't mean that you never defend yourself. I'm personally against violence and avoid it whenever possible, but you will invite more violence upon yourself if you allow abuse. The issue here is AWARENESS and CHOICE. Every interaction is an opportunity to become more awake, more alive and intelligent. Once in a while it may be necessary to flatten some bozo's nose.

History is stained with violence done by those who were "just following orders." Robots cannot be held responsible for their actions, only human beings can. Duty is no excuse for murder. We are all responsible for our actions.

As a CREATIVE REBEL, there is no need to cover up actions with lies. Do the best you can and take full responsibility for the outcome, honestly. If you make mistakes, you know what not to do next time. The burden of guilt is thrown.

It is impossible to become anything other than yourself and existence has chosen you to be here now. Trying to be like someone else is futile, you'll become an actor and chances are you'll fail to even flower as yourself. We all have tremendous potentials which can be fulfilled if we are allowed to discover where these potentials lie.

If there is a reflection in your mirror, then YOU ARE! No matter what you are doing, underneath is a human being. To know that BEING, contacting the life energies flowing through you from existence is the original purpose of all religion. Allowing those energies to flow naturally is the beginning of CREATIVE REBELLION. Awesome, ain't it?

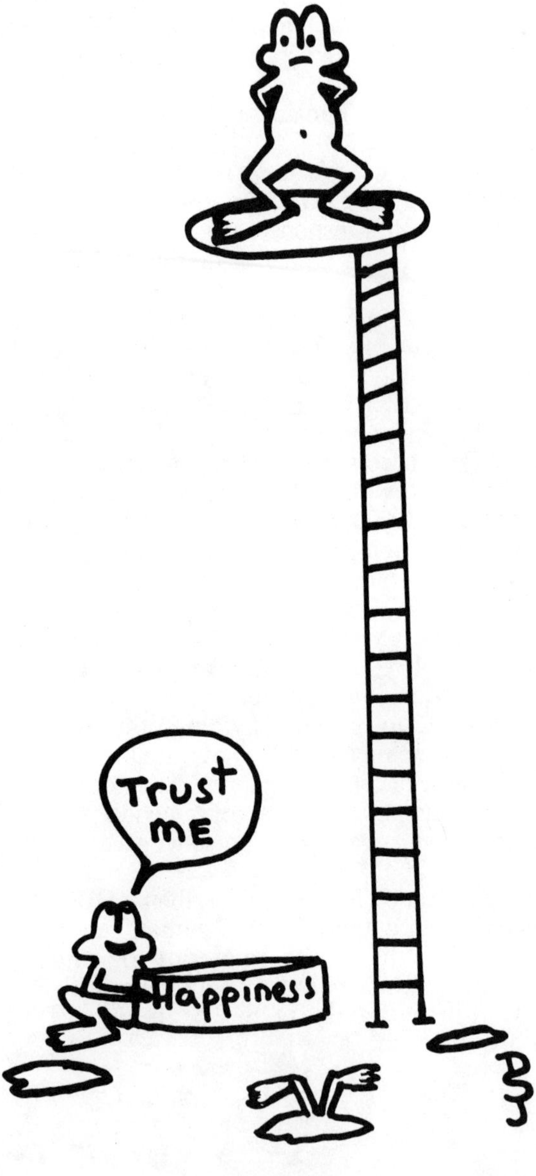
Trust me
Happiness
DJ

CHAPTER TWO

PSYCHOLOGY: ANALYZING DARKNESS

Psychology has been used in one form or another to fit children into almost all societies. "The boogey man will get you" and "You'll be cast into hell fire" have now been replaced with "Maybe we'll have to take you to a psychiatrist." In some cases this can be a positive move, especially if your parents come along. A psychiatrist is trained to shake up old patterns and reveal emotional and communication blocks which can help a home situation greatly.

From my own experience, psychology is a good FIRST step, but can never be a cure-all for every problem. Because it is the art of analyzing the mind with the mind, it lacks the distance needed to reveal the subtle patterns to which the mind clings.

The practice of psychology is based more in hypothesis than in provable fact. Each shrink seems to project the workings of their own minds onto their patients, which explains why there are so many schools of psychology, all arguing for different points of view.

Sigmund Freud, the father of psychoanalysis, obviously wanted to be the father of much more. He kept himself so sexually repressed that he interpreted every dream image as something sexual. He was addicted to cocaine and never allowed himself to be psychoanalyzed so others wouldn't see his own neuroses.

Freud had the insight that most problems relate back to the parents. Unfortunately, those parents picked up their problems from their own parents and on and on. Just seeing this pattern is not enough to break out of it.

Freud used dream interpretation to view the UNCONSCIOUS, or SUBCONSCIOUS, mind. Realizing that rational thought happens only in the conscious mind, he theorized that the subconscious mind sends images as symbols in the deep relaxation of sleep. For example, drowning in a dream may indicate that you are insecure and feel that you are unable to keep afloat in life.

What is this unconscious mind? Are we born with it? No, it is accumulated in this life. Every situation where something happens with which we are unwilling to deal gets stored in the unconscious memory, which is nine-tenths of our physical brain. Even after you consciously forget about the time your daddy took away your teddy bear, the memory may be still lurking in this "mental basement".

Most of the junk stored in the subconscious mind is exactly the things you didn't want others to see. Guilt, feelings of inadequacy, sexual fantasies or perversions and anger are waiting to be unloaded in dreams. This doesn't mean you're a pervert, but that your subconscious is overflowing with repressions. To hold them back is an effort and causes tension so they usually spring out in the relaxation of sleep or when you get inebriated on alcohol. This is the release-valve which keeps you from going totally insane.

Have you noticed that it is usually those who are working at a job they dislike, are involved in a bad marriage or are utterly miserable, who drink often? The ensuing mental diarrhea dumps out enough tension so they can drag themselves on until the next drunk.

Carl Gustav Jung went even deeper than Sigmund Freud, discovering the existence of a COLLECTIVE UNCONSCIOUS mind. He noted that there is common symbology present in most societies, even those who were not in physical contact with each other. He called these symbols ARCHETYPES, and theorized that there is a subtle portion of the mind shared by all human beings collectively and he set out to interpret these archetypes to help him understand the deeper programmings we all carry.

In a riot, the collective mind can be seen to take over individuals. Those who seemed well-adjusted and intelligent before the riot can be seen bashing heads and looting with the crowd. They have been swept up by the collective insanity.

Politicians often use the collective unconscious mind to further their causes. Adolph Hitler, for example, used psychological methods to instill patriotism and hatred of Jews into the collective mind of Germany, leading to World War Two. In his mass rallies, he gathered the young and impressionable to get the movement started, but soon drew millions into this absurd philosophy. By constant repetition delivered to angry people in a state of mass hysteria, Hitler was able to create an army of fanatics, ready to conquer the world and murder innocent Jews without questioning what they were doing.

Jung was on the right track and offered many valuable insights, but he fell short of discovering a still deeper layer of mind called the COSMIC UNCONSCIOUS MIND. Pretty radical stuff! Mentioned only recently in western thought, the East has known of this primary bond of BEING shared by all existence for centuries. Even a rock is connected to the whole on this level.

Then came Alfred Adler. He expanded on the symbolism of the unconscious mind, but decided the major driving force of mind was THE QUEST FOR POWER instead of sex. Again, this may say more about Mr. Adler than about humanity, but there is a valuable insight here. We've all been taught competition in schools, sports and business. It is those who feel weak, probably most of us at one time or another, who become interested in power.

I'll look in detail at the mechanics of POWER in a later chapter, but let me repeat that it is those who feel inferior who wish to be superior. Weakness and fear lead to egoism and power. It takes tremendous strength to enjoy being ORDINARY.

B.F. Skinner was the founder of Behaviorist Psychology. His basic premise was: if behavior is modified, problems disappear. This guy misses the boat from the start in thinking that behavior defines the individual. Skinner was a scientist and disregarded anything he could not see or measure. All the great things of life: love, beauty, freedom, cannot be measured.

Still, Behaviorist Psychology has worked well with some retarded people and others who cannot be reached in any other way. By offering rewards and punishment to direct the behavior of these individuals, they have been able to fit into the "normal" society.

For the rest of us, though, the focus should be on the MOTIVATIONS behind our behavior. Many of us do things we don't really want to do because we try to live up to others' expectations or we're afraid of the consequences of disobeying. Imagine a priest who looks lustfully at a woman or a young boy, but refrains from a seduction. He hasn't committed a crime, but that doesn't make him pure. Behavior is only on the periphery.

Behaviorists have studied the chemicals in the brain which control anger, sex, fear, etc. They found that reducing certain chemicals or adding others radically alters behavior. But, behavior isn't consciousness. Getting rid of the sex drive will only make you impotent, not enlightened.

Now let's look at a real rebel, Wilhelm Reich. He was experimenting with ancient breathing techniques and movement in conjunction with TANTRIC methods from ancient India, which used sexual techniques to create enough energies for religious experience. He also applied his findings to scientific equipment such as his "energy accumulator".

Reich named this dynamic energy of life ORGONE ENERGY. Despite his healing of physical maladies and mental illness, Reich was imprisoned and his books ordered burned by the US government. Some hidden copies are being reproduced now.

R. D. Laing was another rebel who gained widespread opposition from the contemporary psychiatric community. Instead of merely analyzing problems, symbols and past traumas, Laing allowed his patients to FREAK OUT, releasing their insanity. As it continues to evolve, I feel this will be the direction of future psychology, emptying the subconscious mind, thus lifting the tension and returning clarity of vision.

There are many contemporary individuals too numerous to mention who are developing new methods to help us understand ourselves. Elizabeth Kubler-Ross and Steven Levine have opened the realm of death and dying, something Freud, Jung and others dared not mention.

Psychiatric analysis is a process which begins, but is never finished. The human mind has an infinite capacity to create new problems as soon as the old ones are solved. I view psychology as a band-aid, used to patch people up enough to fit them back into the society, but it never reaches the ROOTS of the problem. Usefulness to society is not a valid criterion for mental health.

So, what's missing? There is another level of consciousness called SUPERCONSCIOUSNESS. Actually, it is not even a state of mind, but a pure state of awareness, beyond thoughts and ideas.

The psychologies of the past have been focused on the negative, the unconsciousness and all its layers. To steal a quote from a Bioenergetics teacher, "You can mold it, you can squeeze it, you can break it down into its components and analyze it ... but it's still shit. Learn how to flush it."

When entering a dark room, do you try to SOLVE the darkness? Most likely, you turn on a light. Similarly, the experience of superconsciousness brings light into all the unconscious layers and dissolves them. Unconsciousness only exists because of a lack of awareness.

Labelling mental disorders does not help. Who cares which phobia you have when you're scared? Only by going into the fear with awareness, seeing that the fear has blurred your true vision, can you go beyond it. All fear relates to death and superconsciousness introduces you to the part of yourself that survives death.

How can you experience superconsciousness? It's called MEDITATION. "Oh, no," I hear you saying. "Do I have to chant magic mantras, visualize money falling from the sky or stand on my head with my legs tied around me like a pretzel?" No, these are not meditations. They are mere toys given to those who can't understand watchfulness.

Mantras are repeated sounds which are used to replace the babble of the mind. Unfortunately, you are filling the mind again, with the mantra. It is subtle hypnotism. Some who've played with mantras for years can't even close their eyes without hearing the mantra start up. It is relaxing, but not meditative.

Visualization is based in dreaming. Just by wanting something and imagining it has happened doesn't make it so. It can be valuable in convincing the body to fight diseases, but try visualizing a clear road in a blizzard and you'll see that there are things which are out of your control.

VISUALIZE REALITY!

MEDITATION is the experience of WATCHING, observing your body, thoughts and emotions without judgment. Some techniques will be helpful in getting a glimpse of this potential, but meditation can happen any moment, for no reason at all. In fact, you are doing it right now! Only the association with your mind and its dreams keeps us too involved with personal dramas to be aware of the WATCHER.

Superconsciousness cannot be given to another person. By watching the body, mind and emotions, you know you are not any of these things, otherwise, who is watching? The trick is to become associated with the watcher, instead of the thoughts and actions. This doesn't mean you try to control the thoughts. Allow ideas to go by like passing traffic, but you stand aside and observe without interfering.

There is no training or discipline necessary to meditate. It is not a technique of repressing thoughts and emotions, that will only create more unconsciousness. All that's needed is relaxation with a playful attitude toward life. Accept the way you are and don't try to change, just add awareness. Any changes YOU make can be just as easily unmade. Growth that happens as a natural response to awareness will last forever. This is NEO-PSYCHOLOGY!

CHAPTER THREE

MISERY OR BLISS

By the time you are a teenager, you must be noticing how much MISERY there is in the world. What a mess! If you haven't shut off your feelings and become desensitized, it has to bug the hell out of you. How did misery become the norm? By looking at the roots of misery, we find the key to bliss.

The first notion I'd like to introduce is this: A HAPPY MAN CAN'T BE EXPLOITED. A truly blissful person is not looking for acceptance, more money, salvation or any other goal. His goal is wherever he is right now, like a cat lying in a sunbeam.

An unhappy person can easily be exploited. He's searching for a solution to his problems. He can be fooled by scams to gather wealth, he'll do anything to be accepted and he hopes there's another life because this one has been hell. Exploiters want us all to be unhappy, but how have they been so successful? It's very simple, in a complex sort of way.

Go back to your own childhood. When did you get the most attention? Was it when you were full of laughter, running wildly through the house, screaming with joy? I doubt it. You were probably told, "Shut up, we're reading the paper!"

Most likely, you got more attention when you were sad and crying, or sick. A sad or ill child gets hugged and cuddled, lots to eat and drink, and never has to go to school. With rewards like that, it's a wonder anyone gets healthy again!

I once watched a friend calling her mother. She was feeling fine when she dialed, but her mother kept asking, "What's wrong? You sound ill." My friend actually felt sick by the time she hung up and was crying and feeling sorry for herself. This must have helped the mother to feel NEEDED but it drained my friend's joy.

SYMPATHY is dangerous. It is a cheap substitute for love. Sympathy is negative and sucks the life out of both victim and benefactor. The focus is on illness and self-pity is the result.

LOVE is a totally different phenomenon. Love is positive, coming from the heart as an overflow. There is no need for sympathy and self-pity; love is offered despite the sickness, not because of it. Love does not need to be earned or deserved and it cannot be given on demand.

Seeing that misery is a major source of getting attention, we can now look at misery as an introduction to power. Misery and "miserly" are related words. Only the unhappy want to gather possessions and power. Those with inner riches are able to share without losing anything.

In poor countries, where food and shelter are constantly lacking, it is simple to understand the pain and suffering of the people. Primitive religions must have been born out of desperation, praying for some greater being to bring the food and needs you can't find. Mankind is weak compared to other animals. He can't run very fast, isn't a great fighter, nor can he survive long without food and water.

Being so vulnerable, man's only survival tool is his mind. He created weapons, learned to ride faster animals, invented ways to grow food and store water. Still, deep inside, we know we are weak and will die someday.

DEATH is a journey into the unknown and none can escape it. Because of the fear of death, man has created stories of afterlife, heavens and hells. Every religion has its own stories which contradict each other, but none can prove their claims because, once dead, no one has dropped back in to chat about it.

To tame the wild adventurous spirit of mankind, wise guys invented the concepts of heaven and hell. Through fear of eternal punishment and greed for eternal partying, the churches became powerful and wealthy, supported by thousands of poor people. The rich also donated, knowing the churches kept the poor believing in afterlife, which prevented revolution.

This is the reason Karl Marx declared religion to be the OPIUM OF THE PEOPLE. Beliefs kept the masses pacified, with hopes of a better life after death. No matter how miserable this life was, they wouldn't fight to change it.

The entire modern religious system is based on the nuclear FAMILY. Before families, children had been raised by the entire tribe, with much more freedom and individuality. It was the introduction of personal property that caused the birth of the nuclear family. A man who could own land and accumulate possessions and wealth wanted his accumulations to keep growing, even after his death.

To insure that the children who received the wealth were HIS, marriage was invented. The wife and children became possessions of the man. The churches added the sanctity aspect, as if God was marrying you, because the family was now able to program the children into the church's ideologies. Whatever the religion of the parents became the religion of the children.

The church has been patterned after the same hierarchy with its leaders on the top. Pope means FATHER. God was the ultimate father. He was not introduced as a friend, but as a disciplinarian, watching your every move. If you managed to disobey your parent's rules without them catching you, the God was always watching.

Guilt is a great way to control people because it divides them within, between the way they are told to be and the way they really are. This is psychological warfare. If you masturbate, you feel guilty. If you don't, you feel horny. Either way, you are miserable.

THE SPLITTING OF ADAM

Nature is our reality, the way existence has created us. We all have sex drives, a love of freedom and intelligence. Dividing the individual was the first step in creating the global schizophrenia of today. No one knows himself. If he allows nature, he feels like a SINNER. Everything fun and juicy is condemned. Even a delicious dessert can be called sinful.

So, if everything fun or sensuous brings guilt, what to do? You are told to go to the church and confess your guilt, which is admitting you are wrong. Why should the church forgive you for wanting to be happy? If you've hurt someone, ask for their forgiveness, not the church's. Life becomes so complex when anything comes between us and reality.

If a child has never been programmed to feel guilty, she will never be fooled into a life of suffering. It is because children are conditioned into beliefs long before they are interested in exploring spirituality, that their eyes can never see clearly. A tiny baby can see clearly, with no prejudice, but she has no understanding yet of what she sees. This is why Jesus said we must become like little children again, without ideas and preconceptions, looking with wonder at the world.

When religion has become cerebral, the mind comes in the way of clear vision. A Christian will interpret every event in relation to what he has read in the Bible. Under duress, his mind may project an image of Jesus. A Buddhist will see Buddha; a Muslim will see Mohammed. Has a Christian ever had a vision of Buddha? Impossible. His mind hasn't been trained toward Buddha.

With a concept of God, looking down at you from above, one begins to think that everything that happens to him is a reward or a punishment. This belief keeps people scared and unwilling to allow themselves to have fun, or they will be punished. Maybe life just happens and our part is how we respond to it.

If you come right down to it, most people are very angry. By giving the responsibility of their lives to God, to their bosses, to the society and to a set of moralities, they feel like victims. One way to throw this anger is in watching football, boxing, rollergames, murders on TV and who knows what else? Angry people can cheer when the bad guy gets blown away on the TV. Why? Because the BAD guy doesn't follow the rules and needs to be punished. Subtly, the viewer is jealous.

By now, you must have heard the word SUBLIMATION. Sexually, it means you should find other ways to spend your energy when you feel horny because sex is not acceptable. Very repressed people will get obsessed with gathering wealth and power, hoping a little more money will make them finally happy. Repressed sex causes anger so sports is a good sublimation.

Those who never let themselves go and live totally are the most afraid of death. They may surround themselves with possessions and security forces, do drugs from the doctor to excess, but death will come anyway. Monetary hoarding cannot bring happiness or prevent death.

A LOVER is ready to face death anytime, absolutely penniless. Once the heart has opened and the blissfulness of love vibrates through her being, a deep contentment settles. Lovers cannot be exploited with dreams of power. This moment is so fulfilling, who cares about tomorrow?

In human relationships, most of us have felt the power of love, however momentary. Are you thinking about some guy or girl right now? Feel your heart. Extreme attraction allows the heart to open, but love is irrational and frightening to the rational mind. It may last only a moment or a few days. When it happens, you may dance and sing for no reason at all, making others think your elevator doesn't reach to the top floor. The birds sing back to you, life is good.

Then the mind enters, trying to MAKE IT LAST. As soon as mind comes, the heart closes because these two centers cannot be active at the same time. Thinking about love, writing poetry and planning to be married is a sure sign that the heart has closed again. Love has already died.

Hold on, not all is bad. Mystics have discovered a state of consciousness where love becomes LASTING. It is no longer a desire, or passion and there is no more misery. Love becomes cool and gentle. Even without a lover, the heart remains open and overflows.

The first step toward this STATE OF LOVE is to become happy. Decide what your energies really want to do and try it. Then you'll see if it was just an idea, or a potential you want to grow toward. Painting, dancing, music, designing clothing; start with the dream and investigate it. Don't waste a moment doing what someone else wants you to do.

To check if you are ON THE PATH, see if you're happy. If you know deep in your soul that you are growing and learning to laugh and celebrate life, that's it. If you are certain that you are becoming more of a hypocrite and growing serious, turn around, you're heading away from yourself.

Well-meaning people are constantly telling us to smile, to be nice and to love each other. But love isn't something you can do, or it will be an act, a pretension. Nothing is more ugly than a BLISS BUNNY who pretends to be happy all the time, hiding the reality of changing moods. Be natural.

Love, bliss, meditation and anything beautiful in this world are happenings, not doings. We cannot bring the mysteries of life to ourselves by direct methods. Indirectly, we can prepare the soil for those blossoms to come by being authentic, learning to transform anger and negativity without repressing it, and allowing existence to lead without fighting.

If misery has become the normal state for life on Earth, it is time for REBELLION. Paradise is a state of consciousness, available right here, right now.

CHAPTER FOUR

CLEARING YOUR VISION

There is no possibility of CREATIVE REBELLION without clear vision. Freedom is not just another name for licentiousness. In the sixties, hippies tried drugs, orgies and dropped out of the society thinking it was a declaration of freedom. Although it may have been a great relief to their pent-up emotions, it couldn't last long.

Doing whatever you feel like doing appears to be a sort of freedom, but it lacks one essential quality: FREEDOM FROM ONE'S SELF. Since most of us have been taught the right way to ACT since we were toddlers, we've lost the basic direction of our own potentials. Our minds are clouded with mountains of information gathered from schools, parents, churches and friends so we think we know a lot about life. How much of this KNOWLEDGE has come from our actual experiences? How do we know it's true?

Visual symbols have been used to manipulate us in every way. Flags are used by every country to instill patriotism and a collective ego, separating us from the rest of the world. Religions also use logos such as crosses, Buddha statues, pentagrams, etc. to keep the masses associated with their collective mind-sets.

Television has proven to be one of the most misused technologies of our times. It could have been used to bring beautiful art, music and theater into our homes, as is done mostly on Public Broadcasting Stations.

It even could have been an aid to meditation as was tried by the INTERFACE group in the mid-seventies. They ran visual images through a video synthesizer, producing gorgeous displays of dancing colors. Set to music, these images were shown on talk shows and most callers claimed to be more relaxed and happier after only five minutes of watching this ELECTRONIC ART.

Television could have become a valuable learning aid for children, but only a few educational shows have been produced. Instead of positive or beautiful programming, TV has plunged a nightmarish world of violence, perversion and terror into our living rooms. One recent estimate states that a modern five-year-old has already witnessed over 40,000 TV murders!

Besides murders, there are fights, lies, and the animalistic ways people are shown to LOVE each other. Can anyone dispute that these horrors will have an impact on viewers, especially children who like to mimic what they see.

Even children's shows have changed in recent years into animated versions of adult shows. Tiny kids are watching their heroes inflict violence on others because they are "accepted" villains. The new heroes are not out to prevent violence and crime, but to punish and injure the BAD guys.

Who are the TEENAGE MUTANT NINJA TURTLES and why are they so popular? Because they are cool, free and powerful, they can do whatever they think is right in a world gone mad. All of us wish at one time or another that we could control the injustices and the crimes we see around us, but is violence the answer?

A recent book called MANUFACTURING CONSENT reveals how the evening news is also biased according to the desired effect it is to have on the viewers. They state:

"...the powerful are able to fix the premises of discourse, decide what the general populace will be allowed to see, hear and think about, and 'manage' public opinion by mounting regular propaganda campaigns."[1]

By giving intense news coverage to the stories which are aligned with the accepted TRUTH of the status quo, the masses are manipulated into acceptance or hatred. Acceptable victims, like the casualties of Bhagdad, get little coverage, while unacceptable victims, like hostages, are used to sway public opinion and designate selected enemies.

Hours of television coverage were dedicated to the earthquake in San Francisco and it continued for weeks. Certainly it was a horrible disaster, but almost no coverage is given to the 40,000 children who starve to death EACH DAY in third world countries. If over-population is depicted in its actual magnitude, viewers would be swayed to support birth control, to which the Fundamentalists in government are opposed.

Blacks, Hispanics and women are often ignored by the media except for token gestures. Note how many cop shows cast minorities as criminals. What kind of message does this send to minority kids? Is this supposed to be their future?

Television limits viewers to being spectators instead of doers. Many are content to watch others live, fall in love, create artwork, etc. It may be safer than going through it yourself, but what kind of life do you have? They say your life flashes before you at the moment of death; most people will be seeing reruns of I LOVE LUCY in place of their own lives.

In Junior High School, I refused to watch any TV. When I heard members of my family walking through the house singing jingles from commercials, I knew I didn't want my brain to be bombarded

---

[1] Herman and Chomski, 1989

with this subtle brainwashing, and I still don't. Advertisers know that flashing neon signs make you read their messages again every time the sign lights up, and repetitive commercials can plant their products into your subconscious mind without your knowing.

CLEARING VISION means dropping all borrowed knowledge, escaping from given prejudices and judgments so we can inquire into reality without limitation. The mind stops projecting expectations onto every event and labels onto every object. Perceptions and feelings are actually heightened when thoughts stop distracting them from encountering reality.

The Biblical story of the GARDEN OF EDEN is a metaphorical statement of everyone's childhood. Before our minds get clouded with KNOWLEDGE, we are in a sort of paradise, unseparated from the world around us. For nine months, we have floated in bliss in the womb and we now look with wonder at the colorful world around us.

When language is introduced, we tend to label things and are separated from the direct experience. Adults think in language. When encountering a willow tree blowing in the breeze, they will say, "It's a willow tree, how beautiful." The viewer is separated from the viewed and the label BEAUTIFUL keeps our energies in the mind, instead of melting into the experience of beauty. Paradise is lost. Language is necessary for communication, but a side effect is that we begin to gather information about things we don't really know.

Watch how a child explores a tree. She touches it, smells it, sees it as if for the first time, each time. It is not labelled as a willow tree, but seen as THIS amazing living thing. Meeting a willow tree in this manner, you may want to sit beneath it and feel its energies (or maybe make out with your girl or boyfriend.) It is a first meeting, not to be missed.

CLEAR VISION is already the case at birth, but a baby is totally ignorant. Soon the mind gets stuffed with DOs and DON'Ts and we learn to be cunning in the ways of the world to succeed. There is no way around it, but there is a chance to return to innocence and clear vision, by choice instead of ignorance. By seeing the damage cunningness does, we choose to be trusting again.

TRUST is not faith. Trust means that you can see that life is taking care of you, breathing in you, beating in your heart, whether you deserve it or not. Life showers on all. Naturally things happen that you don't like and weren't expecting, but a deep acceptance enters into your being. Things just happen. Don't take it all personally, it isn't only punishment and reward. Life is a huge phenomenon with so many overlapping events and characters that it is impossible, and unnecessary, to understand it all.

"Life is not a problem to be solved. It is a mystery to be lived."[2] Problems arise when trust dies and people try to control everything. Most people live in a strict routine, eating at a certain time, sleeping when they are supposed to, watching the same TV shows ... UGH! Why not eat when you get hungry and sleep when you're tired? Why this need to control? Existence lets us know when to eat. This is acceptance.

Seeing things clearly and accurately is simple. It doesn't require years of study to see what is needed in life. Knowledge without experience creates veils of prejudice.Once you've experienced something directly, no one can fool you into believing lies. No doctrines and teachings are needed to set you on the path. Take a step in any direction, there is YOUR path. You are one with the mystery.

The CREATIVE REBEL needs no beliefs. Do you need to believe in the Earth? No, it's really here and you see her every day. Only fictions require beliefs and faith. Follow each belief you've been carrying to its source and you will probably find an ulterior motive, someone wants to exploit you. Beliefs are invented to control you. Only GOOD children go to heaven.

So, here we are as teenagers with our heads already filled to the brim with chopped liver. I have observed teenage girls who've shaved their heads and wear safety pins through their noses as a protest to the society, but they still wear makeup and shave their legs! The society remains within.

To fit into our so-called civilized society, we've learned to hide our anger, fears, hatreds, weaknesses. All this baggage is stored in the subconscious mind and we need to constantly hold it back. Even a small incident will bring an outburst of pent-up emotions, right? To purposely release these emotions without hurting anyone else will instantly bring clearer vision.

One of my favorite techniques is to sit quietly and see whatever idea pops into my mind and trace it to the source, where did I pick up this idea? Was it a parent, teacher, TV, a friend or enemy, a book, who was it I trusted enough to accept this idea? Is this idea actually true? It may be true, but the question here is, do I know from my own experience? If not, I drop that belief.

Many parents prevent children from making their own mistakes and learning from experience. By telling children that everything is

[2] Bhagwan Shree Rajneesh

dangerous, they keep kids in fear and dependent on their decisions instead of learning for themselves. Let kids fall down! They'll get up and learn how to walk on their own.

A child who is warned that a candle flame is HOT, and allowed to experiment anyway will discover the truth of it and will understand the warning not to play in the street. An over-protected child will never learn to be responsible and will always need BAILING OUT. This may keep the parents feeling needed but the child is crippled.

Millions of people believe things their whole lives and later find out they have been proven false, but never suspect that MOST of their beliefs may also be false. Ultimately, we have to come to a point where we ask, "Do I really KNOW anything at all?" One more step and we may realize that it isn't necessary to know everything, or to pretend that we do.

Knowledge gives us the false idea that we are safe, in control of life. In reality, life happens with or without us, but our responses are clearly up to us. Ideas lead us into the future or back into the past, missing the only reality, here and now. In becoming free of our own minds, we can see reality and deal with life out of our clarity.

I've participated in many SPIRITUAL THERAPY groups and one common theme stood out. Each participant was there to break through the walls he'd created around himself to allow others to see his reality. After discovering what he was hiding, a tearful participant once asked, "Why am I like this?"

It seems like a valid question. Why are we doing things we don't really want to do and hurting those we love? The group leader took off his shoe and held it out. "I'm going to drop this shoe," he said. "Just watch me. I hate this shoe and I refuse to hold it any longer." Still he held the shoe and waited for a response.

Not understanding, the participant cried again, "But why do I manipulate people and hurt them?"

Again the therapist threatened to drop the shoe. The tearful man finally laughed, the shoe was dropped. There is no need to work things out that are not real, but only ideas. Behavior is like clothing, we wear it. Just seeing the way we are ACTING gives us a chance to stop acting. There doesn't need to be any effort to change, seeing clearly is enough and changes happen naturally.

Since most of our emotional problems have roots in the distant past, it's easy to throw the responsibility and say, "My parents screwed me up, it's their fault. What can I do ..." Yeah, yeah, we all know that one. It may well be the fact, that problems in the family get focused on the "black sheep", the misfit of the family. We may even act as thermometers, picking up hidden tensions in the household and acting them out. The problems may not be ours, but we may be the most sensitive family members, thus exploding from the tensions around us.

Still, the fact is that right now, there are no problems clinging to us, we are holding onto them like they are valuable diamonds. We worry that we'll lose our identity if we lose our problems. Lose them! Sure, it's painful to let go of past traumas, but only at first. To release the pain, we have to relive it and be finished with it. If we've put off grieving for a lost relative or pet because it hurts too much, those psychological memories continue to haunt our subconscious minds and the pain remains, possibly keeping us from loving others because we fear more pain.

Regressive techniques are often easier to do with a group of friends, all helping each other to become free of the past. It takes tremendous courage to allow others to see your private fears and weaknesses but, seeing they still accept you, you begin to trust again. Social Services Departments often can help a family to bring out their fears, angers and tensions into the open, so one person doesn't go crazy being the "Identified Patient".

Until you clean out the cobwebs from your mind, don't have too much faith in your perceptions of reality. Who knows how much toxic waste has been dumped in your attic? Have a yard sale and get free of all the junk. Regressive therapies like Primal, Encounter and Bioenergetics are needed at first, but cannot be the end. You can clear out the garbage, but it is still cold and dark in there. Now the cleared space needs LIGHT.

Since teenagers don't have much investment in the society and the lies it uses to control people, you are more open to recognize and embrace the truth. Remember though that truth is always changing, just like time, and you have to remain open and available to each moment to live a life of truth.

No matter how much clutter is dumped out, the mind has an infinite capacity to gather more junk. A separation from the workings of the mind is needed. Mind is like a child who needs your attention constantly, calling, "Mommy, watch me!" The more you feed it attention, the crazier it gets.

Taking a simple step backward into your WATCHER, from where you can observe, without judgment, the workings of the mind, is MEDITATION. You can't force it, but it comes with expanding awareness. Soon, by itself, the radio in the back of your head will stop blasting commercials and peace will fill your being.

With clear vision, you can no longer be AGAINST the society. You may be right in the middle of the business world or living high in the mountains. Either way, fighting is over and you can be yourself, wherever you choose to be.

THE WATCHER

CHAPTER FIVE

FINDING YOUR SELF

Where do you look to find yourself? A mirror? That's a good place to start. In a way, we are all mirrors of each other. As individuals, we have evolved various personal characteristics, but collectively, we are all representatives of humanity.

Whenever we see something in another that we don't like, it is usually some trait we see in ourselves that we can't accept. Conversely, those traits we adore in others are the parts of ourselves we admire. With this in mind, there is no reason to condemn anyone or demand that they try to change. Every meeting with another can become an opportunity to learn more about ourselves.

Human beings have almost all become hypocrites. To return to authenticity is difficult. As children, we learn that truth is punished so we learn to lie to avoid punishment. Getting caught seems to be the real problem. Parents continuously tell their children to be honest, but then spank them if the truth comes out.

How many parents are honest? I've witnessed parents telling their children to lie on the phone, pretending that they are not at home. The whole society uses lies in political elections, influencing others and keeping their own reality hidden. Children get the idea that lies are acceptable as long as they work.

Most adults can't admit to children that they themselves are ignorant. Instead of admitting that they don't know something, they force the same beliefs they were taught, as if they were factual. This teaches children to hide their weaknesses and faults as they see the parents doing. With continuous repetition, we start to believe that we really are the masks we show others in a subtle form of self-brainwashing.

Santa Claus, the Easter Bunny, the Tooth Fairy, all these lies create a situation where parents won't be trusted later. Knowing that your parents are hypocrites makes it impossible to expose your reality to them.

We are molded into patterns of thought about race, religion, gender, family, country, city and all kinds of other false identities. We know ourselves through these demarcations instead of encountering our realities. No wonder no one knows who she is, we've all been pulled outward.

So, lets go inward again, back to this MEDITATION stuff. It isn't really a DOING at all, just observing. Since watching is already happening, it's merely a change of quality, of new awareness.

"Okay, man, that sounds easy. I'm pretty lazy," you might be saying. Let's try. Sit right down in a comfortable position and close your eyes. (Better read the instructions first.) Now, stop thinking for thirty minutes, not ONE thought about that cute girl or boy you have a crush on. Ready? GO!

*

* * *

* * * * *

* * * * * * * * * *

Back so soon? That certainly wasn't thirty minutes, but it must have been enough time to prove that you can't just sit down and stop your mind. That sweetheart of yours was there constantly, renting your top floor.

And it wasn't only one thought that came, was it? A thousand-and-one ideas came to demand your attention. Did you finish your school work? What's on TV? What's for dessert? Notice that your mind wasn't filled with all this garbage until you tried to stop it.

This is exactly the reason people choose not to meditate. It makes them aware of the insanity in their heads, which wasn't noticed when they were keeping busy all the time. Playing ostrich won't dissolve the insanity.

This mind is a TRICKY device. Although amazingly well suited to deal with the outside world, sensations, analysis, communications and computing, there is no switch to turn it off. Everything you see invites the mind to comment on something similar it has seen in the past. If you're a total geek, you can actually tell others your stories of, "The last time I did this." You may not have many friends this way.

When it's not dragging you into the past, the mind shows sneak previews of the future it hopes to see. Daydreams can be a handy device to escape from your Algebra class, but they never come true the way you imagined anyway. Worst of all, you are missing your life, which is only happening NOW.

In Japan, there are little dolls which illustrate the difference between meditators and intellectuals. The intellectual dolls have huge heads, and always fall down. The meditator dolls have big hearts and bellies and can't be rolled over.

The mind is a great servant, but should not become the master. We need to move our energies from the intellect into the heart and then deeper into the BEING to discover our reality. Sitting in the corner quietly like the monks of old will only prove to you that you are crazy, planning for the future, dreaming of the past.

No wonder everyone is afraid of death if they never are HERE to live this life. Even when people finally get that vacation they've been dreaming of for months, they lie on the beach and think about going back to work! Gross me out!

How can we come back to NOW? This has been the puzzle for all the mystics, how to pull the victim of his own mind back into the present, into the HEART, then into the BEING. Then time stops. It is always NOW. The first question is: Are you finished dreaming yet? Do you want to wake up? If not, at least stop snoring so loudly so the rest of us can enjoy breakfast.

There are thousands of methods invented to snap the mind from its dreams and maybe only one will work for you. The good news is that all those methods revolve around one basic concept, learning to WATCH. "Trying" to relax will bring in the mind and tension and keep you from relaxing. Very frustrating.

But wait, there are easy ways. You don't have to isolate yourself in a cave for twenty years staring at the bats. Since we have become so computer-like in our minds, we need MOVING meditations like dancing, running, jumping or riding a bicycle. All these activities move our energies to a peak and throw off tensions. As a result, relaxation happens naturally, immediately following the action. After any heavy physical exercise, FREEZE, look inside.

Meditation is not like TUMS. You can't space out unconsciously for 23 hours a day and suddenly become conscious for one. Every action can become meditative if you bring all your awareness to it, without daydreaming. You can feel the difference between sweeping the floor to get it over with, and being consciously in the hands that are artfully moving the dirt with grace and totality.

It is a KNACK. You can't force it to happen, but you can easily prevent it. Even the realization that you have just slipped into emptiness and silence is enough to disturb it.

At first, you will only get small glimpses. Don't beat yourself up and get greedy for more. The right attitude is to celebrate. After all these years of living like a robot, you have remembered to be here. This celebrative attitude invites the silence to come again.

A light and playful person can meditate easily. That's why it is important to remove most of the major stresses from your mind before trying to sit quietly. Put aside all that vastly important trivia and freeze like a statue, then just FEEL.

You want another technique which is fun? Okay. The Russian Master George Gurdjieff invented the STOP technique. It's very simple, but very powerful. Every time you see that you have forgotten to be here again, freeze where you are for thirty seconds. This abrupt halt catches the mind off guard and you'll soon feel something unworldly descending on you. The mind needs movement to jump from idea to idea and the freezing of the body helps break that insane busy-ness.

IMPORTANT NOTE: In case there are any dummies reading this, please don't attempt this technique while driving a car or doing anything dangerous.

Between any two thoughts, there is a silent GAP. We don't usually see these gaps because our focus is on the thoughts. By watching these gaps, they grow longer. The mind gets a rest and your consciousness gets the energy usually spent on thinking. A time comes when the gaps become a continuum and the mind only gets used when you need it.

Please don't take my word for it. Try it. Finding your SELF is its own reward. Spiritual experience comes in waves. Sometimes you'll know you are getting close and other times you'll know you are light years away from yourself. When up, celebrate and share your joy with others. When down, keep to yourself, rest and wait for the next wave to come.

A gnarly little story: In ancient times, man used to assail God with so much whining, so many prayers for this or that, that God was going crazy. He called all his angels together to ask for advice. They all tried to think of places for God to hide, but they knew man would eventually discover every planet. Finally, one angel thought of the perfect spot. Since that time, God has been hiding in the last place a human being would look, in the center of his being.

CHAPTER SIX

DRUGS: THE SHORTCUT TO NOWHERE

Of all the things in the universe, why is there a war on drugs right now? There are many reasons. Drugs are an integral part of our lifestyle, both legal and illegal.

Drugs, meaning mixtures of chemicals, are everywhere in the body. Chemicals are manufactured by the body for every imaginable purpose and life would be impossible without them. Mankind has learned to reproduce many of these chemicals from plant and mineral sources to affect the body in many ways.

Drug ABUSE begins when narcotics and inebriates are used to escape from problems or relieve boredom. The problems remain, in fact they multiply by our ignoring them.

Mind altering drugs have been in demand since the first Cro-Magnon man chomped on a Datura leaf. Herbal drugs have been used constantly for divination and healing long before modern medicine learned to isolate the constituents, making our modern drugs more sophisticated and powerful.

If people are unhappy and choose to do a pill to get relief, what's all the fuss about? The drugs which concern most people aren't just pills which make you feel better. Addictive drugs, both physical and mental, cease to be fun very quickly, reducing the user to a slave.

Larger quantities are soon needed just to reduce the pain of withdrawal, but withdrawal is unavoidable unless the user dies first of an overdose.

Drugs like crank, methamphetamines, keep the body and mind overstimulated for long periods of time. Exhaustion is inevitable as many vitamins and minerals are sapped from the system, and the mind finally blows a fuse. Smokable forms like ICE can cause violent reactions with nightmarish consequences and has been known to stop the heart.

The Peruvian Indians have chewed Coca leaves for centuries to relieve symptoms of hunger and fatigue. It is a free pain reliever in a poor and short-lived existence. The substances made from Coca leaves which hit the streets of the United States are hundreds of times stronger and more debilitating. Modern research shows that even small doses of cocaine can damage the heart.

Coke is an excellent way to waste your money and your life. The new smokable form, Crack, is proving to be a killer in more ways than one. Besides the fact that it injures many organs of the body, it can make users psychotic and violently insane. The money which goes with its sales can be reason for murder.

Another ancient drug with new problems is OPIUM. It comes in a variety of synthesized forms including codeine, heroin, morphine and many pill forms. For immense pain, as is suffered in war or auto accidents, there is nothing better for short periods, but it is highly addictive and very expensive. I've witnessed middle-class American families, who had been my friends, transformed into vicious, deadly junkies, ready to kill for their next FIX.

Addictive drugs which relieve pain and offer temporary euphoria are rampant in ghettos and other poor areas where people suffer daily. Those who can least afford them have the greatest demand for them. Because these drugs are illegal, they remain expensive, and crime is the destiny of most addicts.

When drug addiction was mainly centered in poor Black and Hispanic areas, little government help was offered. Now hard drugs have sneaked into middle and upper-class homes and politicians are jumping on the bandwagon, crying for a war on drugs in hopes of getting more votes.

It is peculiar to me that no one is interested in WHY so many people are using drugs, but are only interested in punishing them. I feel that the majority of people will continue to use some form of drugs as long as they are unhappy, living lives that they never chose.

Obsessions are many: running for office, gathering wealth, eating to excess, jogging, watching TV, reading books; anything can become a crutch to keep us from remembering the emptiness inside and the fear of death. The desire to escape from life is because no one is living his own life. Drugs are used by those who can't meditate. Anyone who has learned to drop stress and to sit quietly for at least a period of the day, doing nothing but feeling the exquisite energies of life flowing through her will only be brought down by drugs. Getting HIGH on drugs only proves that you are very low. Drugs that desensitize, so miserable people can escape from themselves, will only take meditators away from their bliss.

All drugs are not alike. Psychedelic drugs like LSD, psilocybe mushrooms, and peyote are not addictive and can open the subconscious mind to the conscious mind. Unfortunately, there are many things stored in the subconscious mind which you might not be ready to see, so psychedelics can plunge the user into a day of constant nightmares. A BAD TRIP can really shake you up and the mind can flip into flashbacks for years after.

Meditation, as I've said before, is just watching. If psychedelic drugs are ingested by a meditator, he can watch the mind from a distance, not being identified with the images released. A meditator has already looked into the subconscious mind and can reach these same spaces without drugs which harm the body.

WARNING: Most psychedelics purchased on the streets are laced with impurities, like rat poison, which can cause permanent and recurring health problems. These are not the pure forms tried by Timothy Leary, Richard Alpert, Aldous Huxley, John Lily and others back when they were legal. It is important to note that all these drugs are now illegal and can cost you your most important value --- Freedom.

Looking at the TV, you might wonder why politicians are screaming to lock up drug dealers when big drug companies are trying to sell the most powerful forms of legal drugs to anybody who wants to buy them. How can we drag kids to jail for smoking a joint when millions of Americans are addicted to LEGAL drugs and alcohol?

Tons of legal drugs are taken every day, coffee to wake up, aspirin, acetaminophen and ibuprofen for pain, alcohol to unwind and a sleeping pill to go to sleep. Doctors supply valium and other prescription drugs for pain. But pain is the way our bodies tell us that something is wrong, so why take the phone off the hook instead of trying to solve the problem?

Acceptable drugs like tobacco and caffeine stimulate the adrenal glands, giving a quick pick-up. After years of abuse, the adrenals wear out or lose the ability to create adrenaline when needed. Cancer is a reward for abusing nicotine and caffeine.

What is the root cause of addiction to stimulants like these? Obviously, there is a lack of energy. Children seem to have plenty of energy, so what has cut that energy during the growth process? Many doctors agree that the return of energy can help kick a stimulant habit.

Poor eating habits may be the leading cause of low energy levels. Businesspeople eat on the run, often overdosing on junk foods, red meats and never taking time to relax for good digestion. I experimented with dozens of diets over the years and can recommend one called THE RATIONAL DIET of Stuart Wheelright.[3] This diet doesn't limit the foods we all love to eat, it combines them correctly for proper digestion and energy. In a nutshell, eat proteins at breakfast with vegetables and eat carbohydrates in the evening. Within a week, I felt twice the energy.

Other helpful energy builders are wheatgrass juice, vegetable juices and Bluegreen algae. These not only clean the system, but

[3] Available from Systemic Formulas, PO Box 1516, Ogden, Utah, 84402

build the body in many ways. Books or information about these can be found at your local healthfood store.

Another great killer of natural energy is being cooped up in a classroom for seven hours a day in school. Most American kids don't get enough exercise. Part of the lesson we learn by sitting all day is to be calm and learn discipline. We can't scream or yell, which are very natural forms of expression.

Wilhelm Reich, the martyred American scientist, discovered that breathing techniques can bring us back much of the energy of youth. We have been taught to breath shallowly, keep ourselves in control. Bioenergetics is a series of techniques based on Reichian therapies which loosen the blocks we have developed in childhood and since.

Now to take on alcohol. It seems that booze addiction is rampant among teenagers. It is legal, to those over a certain age, and easy to obtain. Once in while, it's fun to get a bit tipsy and throw off some of your inhibitions and stored emotions. It becomes a problem only when you can't stop drinking, you drink too often or you drink while driving. Drinking and driving is the major cause of teen-related deaths in our country.

If you want to grow old and sick quickly, alcohol is the right thing. Your body will develop problems which normal people shouldn't see until they're retired. Addiction causes exhaustion, malnutrition, and eventually the DTs.

Those who've become actors, thinking that "Men don't cry" or "I'm always a nice person" may explode when alcohol relaxes their controls on these repressions. Conversely, a meditator who has dealt with life as it comes, without repressing or acting, might get very quiet or giggly when drinking.

The Russian Master, Gurdjieff used to get his disciples totally drunk to see what masks they were hiding behind. This gave him insights into what each person needed to wake up.

Another reason people do drugs is boredom BOREDOM is another symptom of not living your life totally. Whether you've been too frightened to take risks and follow your heart or you've been forced into a lifestyle you didn't choose, it is now up to you. Do you have enough guts to live your life? Others can't choose for you, even if they all think they can.

MARIJUANA creates laziness, lethargy and eventually lung problems. It does not make people violent and a life of crime is not usually associated with pot. The drawback is that constant use will take your life away, either in dreams, or in jail.

The prisons of this country are filled with drug users, yet those same prisons are full of drugs. What gives? Why are people who are using soft drugs to escape from their misery being thrown into jail, where there are hard drugs?

Why do some of us get obsessed with food and develop eating disorders? Part of the problem is that we listen to others and try to live up to their expectations. Food is necessary for life and eating should be a natural process, whenever there is hunger.

Women are often taught that their only value is in their BEAUTY. This places much pressure on women to remain thin, as is appreciated in our culture. An internal war begins between overeating, trying to fill the emptiness inside, and not eating, trying to compete with other women for the attention of men. If weight is gained, she feels like a loser. If weight is lost, she suffers from not eating and may be obsessed with food until the weight is gained again.

Let's stop this game right here. Women have to be liberated from their conditionings. All human beings, male and female, have great potentials and beauty is an inherent quality of a happy person, plump or thin. Have you noticed how ugly a pretty girl can become by overuse of makeup? The very effort to force beauty kills the natural beauty. Be yourself!

Neither the emptiness inside can be filled with food nor does being skinny make one beautiful. Anorexics and bulimics are not healthy-looking or happy. Beauty comes from within, when you are doing whatever it is that nurtures you, that sparks your creativity. Don't let the quest for beauty become another drug. Eat naturally.

As the threat of the Soviet Union diminishes, we have seen thousands of soldiers coming home, without jobs. Is it merely a coincidence that the DRUG WARS started around that time? Fighting drugs may be an excuse to build up a police state in an attempt to take away many of our Constitutional rights. Underground investigators are constantly proving that government employees, including politicians, have been smuggling drugs into our country which makes the drug wars seem to be only an attempt to wipe out their competition.

When Iraq became a new enemy, the government drug wars relaxed a bit. Still, the modern drugs which steal your mind and heart are causing deaths in the streets as drug gangs shoot each other and innocent passers-by. Don't die for drugs!

If you have a drug problem and want to get rid of it, you'll have to discover the beauty within first. To just stop doing addictive drugs COLD TURKEY will be self-torture. You'll be dreaming of the drugs, making it impossible to meditate or enjoy life. By looking inward while under the influence of the drug you're trying to stop, you can find the watcher, the one who isn't affected by the drugs at all. With practice, a warmth and clarity will develop and the drugs will fall away without an intense fight.

As with anything I examine in this book, YOU have to decide whether you are going to do drugs or not. I'm not a preacher. I simply look at the facts and decide what I feel is best for me. From my point of view, no one can be totally free who has a drug habit, and I am against all slavery.

A CREATIVE REBEL cannot be a slave to anybody or anything. With awareness comes sharpness, intelligence. When you find the right thing in life, the thing your entire being wants to do, you'll be too busy creating to mar your vision again with drugs. Once meditation brings joy and self-love, only an idiot will get addicted to drugs.

The craving for drugs shows that something is MISSING in your life. By desensitizing, you forget that something is missing, but the void remains. If you have enough guts, enter the void within and find the center, and cravings for drugs will vanish. It was YOU who was missing!

PS- Telephone number for The National Center For Drug Abuse
1 800 662-HELP toll free.

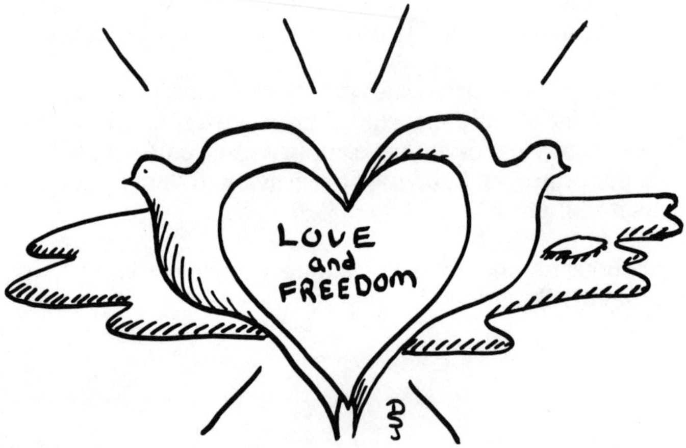
LOVE
and
FREEDOM

CHAPTER SEVEN

SEX, LOVE AND ...

Now here's an interesting topic. Gets your attention right away, doesn't it? But why should sex be more interesting than any other subject? Why is it the major theme of TV, used to sell everything from cars to soda-pop? The reason sex has become a national obsession is that it has been condemned and repressed.

Sex is merely the method nature uses to reproduce the species. If there was not a powerful drive for sex, who would bother to go through all those acrobatics just to make more screaming kids? All beings, except maybe amoebas, would vanish from the Earth without powerful chemical drives to reproduce.

As with anything important, nature has not left the sex drive to the choice of the individual. If you had to remember to breathe, to think about digestion, to consciously attack germ invaders, you would most likely goof off and die. Sex drive is also beyond control and choice, making it an unconscious drive.

Because it is unconscious, it makes us feel a little helpless because no one wants to be a slave, not even to his own desires. This gives a basis to understand the modern sexual obsession. Energy builds in your sex drive beyond your control, so anyone wanting to make you feel guilty has found the ultimate weapon.

Organized religions have jumped on this fact and condemned sex, knowing well it is a powerful force beyond your choice. They make it a SIN to even think about sex, but even condemning it is thinking about it. Since every person is sexual, every follower will feel guilty and think the DEVIL is driving them into sin.

If sex is really a sin, then every flower is heading toward hell, every bird is singing songs of sin and all animals should go to the priests and repent. Churches reserve sinning for human beings because they are the only ones who can be conned into trying to control natural drives. If nature is an enemy, who is responsible for creating these drives in us?

What kind of God creates people with powerful sex drives and then sends messengers to condemn sex? It seems sadistic. Why wouldn't this God like his sons and daughters to enjoy the act of creating new life? Why didn't he make us all perfect, like amoebas? It is BECAUSE God, or existence, has made us all powerfully sexual that religions have used sex to create guilt in us. Anyone feeling guilty becomes divided between the reality of lust and the teaching of chastity. This is how sex has become obsessive. Split people are miserable and miserable people go to church and give money for redemption. What a business!

Sexual energy gets perverted when you fight with it. Those who don't allow their natural sex drives find their dreams filled with sex, are attracted to magazines with photos of naked women and men and are more prone to sadistic and masochistic sexual practices because there is self-hatred associated with sex.

Even Mahatma Ghandi, who tried for most of his life to be celibate, reported constant sexual dreams, even in his old age. He became so anti-life that his disciples had to burn their tongues so they wouldn't enjoy eating tasty foods.

Many recent news stories tell of priests who've forced small children to have sex with them. Homosexuality is widespread in convents and monasteries and many priests are trying to get the churches to declare that homosexuality is not a breach of their vows of celibacy.

I am not for or against homosexuality. That is the freedom of the individual, but many priests turn toward other men only because they are afraid they will go to hell if they are with women. Nuns choose other women because that is their only choice. That is a wrong reason to be homosexual. If you fall in love with someone who has the same gender as you, that is your freedom. But adults forcing sex on children is a sure sign that repression causes obsession.

The condemnation of sex has also been a major factor in the condemnation of WOMEN. Millions of women have been burned to death by religious fanatics, accused of having sex with the devil and being WITCHES. They were forced to admit their guilt under extreme torture. If they survived the torture, it was considered proof that they were witches and they were murdered.

Who were these women who were murdered, mostly during the Inquisition? History shows that many were midwives and herbal doctors, who administered medicines made from plants. Their crime was clear, to protect the lives of other women, who were bred constantly like cattle, the witches discovered herbal methods of birth control.

The word WITCH originally meant WISE WOMAN, but the churches changed the meaning into something evil. It is likely that these witches were metaphysical scientists who knew more about reality than the churches and were murdered to prevent their knowledge from influencing converts. Why have women been singled out for this hatred?

Historically, women have been treated as property of the men, abused and scorned, raped or placed on a pedestal. Chivalry was a golden cage which was used to keep women enslaved by idolizing them. Up on the pedestal, the woman will have to display all the VIRTURES dictated to her, acting weak and unintelligent to make the men feel strong and needed. Gag me with a ball and chain!

Even the Biblical name for the first woman, EVE, seems to have derived from EVEL, the Middle English word for evil. This hatred of women comes because women are beautiful, thus arousing the hated sexual desire in repressed men.

Psychologically, men are more mind-oriented, while women are naturally centered more in the heart. Men tend to THINK about sex, while women FEEL love. Repressed sexual energies often become anger, which is another release for that energy. Every army knows not to let the male soldiers mix with women. If they are too content with life, they will not be good killers.

Most religious orders are restricted to men only. Just seeing a woman causes a volcano of repressed sexuality to erupt. Instead of seeing the fact that enforced celibacy is unnatural, the monks and priests blame women, calling them demons and seductresses. Monks in India have reported being visited by APSARAS, female spirits who try to seduce them from their path. This is the revenge of the mind when nature is perverted.

Sex is not a problem in itself. Just because it is an unconscious drive doesn't mean you can't bring consciousness into it. The meeting of two beings, mingling and dancing together can be healing to both, if guilt does not arise. Modern birth control methods have freed women from having unexpected children and a lifetime of mandatory service.

Now the plot thickens. AIDS has entered the scene and is spreading at an alarming rate on campuses and in inner cities, especially from men to women. It is not worth contracting a deadly disease just for a few moments of pleasure. Many teens who are just starting out sexually don't think about AIDS, and some now have it.

Use of a condom is one way to reduce the chances of contracting AIDS but they are not foolproof. On Jan. 8,1988, the San Francisco Chronicle reported that the US government had cut research funds for a UCLA study on the effectiveness of condoms in halting the spread of AIDS because, "condoms may be incapable of providing reliable protection to participants in the study." It seems that rubber may contain holes as large as 5 microns, while the virus can be 1/10th of a micron.

Having sex with only one partner adds more security but both partner should be tested for antibodies prior to intercourse. These tests are free in most cities and are confidential. Doctors still disagree if kissing is a possible way to transmit AIDS through mouth sores or bleeding gums, but why take a chance? There are so many ways to enjoy the company of another without kissing.

Love is for sharing beauty, not killer diseases. If you don't already know, condoms are available in any drugstore, even in supermarkets and in many men's rooms. Instructions are included.

Don't be in a rush to have sex. I've heard young girls worrying that they are still virgins. Ridiculous! Wait for the right time and the right person. Take the right precautions so you won't have to worry about having a baby or getting AIDS. Be responsible for yourself.

Sex should never be used as a political tool to make others like you or to be accepted as COOL. With a wrong start, your entire sexual lifetime may become a series of manipulative peripheral affairs instead of an intimate meeting of lovers.

In the past, pregnancy was the main fear which prevented girls from experimenting with boys. Modern birth control methods should have eliminated this problem, but teenage pregnancy is on the rise. Girls who've never even been free from school and living with their parents are tied down to eighteen years of motherhood and, often, poverty. What's with you guys?

This unnecessary problem may be partly caused by parents of teens who don't accept the fact that their sons and daughters are sexual. Any conscientious parent will make sure that their teens know about adequate birth control methods. A parent who's too embarrassed to discuss sex with a teenager is inviting disaster.

Bringing consciousness into sex was the focus of TANTRA, the ancient Indian religion. Life energy builds in us as we eat and process food. Sex is the most basic way that energy can be used, but it is only a momentary bliss, and the energy is gone.

Tantra tries to initiate this energy sexually, but then allows it to rise into the heart as LOVE and eventually sparks the higher centers of consciousness. Then sex is used as a door to mystical experience, not an unconscious drive to make babies.

Love does not need intercourse. Sometimes it is beautiful to just lie together, heart to heart, getting excited without throwing the energy away. This can build love as the energy moves up to the heart, then to the consciousness.

The peak of the Tantric experience is when the heart opens naturally, without a lover even present, tuning into the universal love of existence. By bringing consciousness into sex, it is transformed toward superconsciousness.

What would happen if sex were not forbidden? There are tribes who allow their teenagers to have sex as soon as they are of age. These natural tribes don't suffer from the many curses of repression. They have no divorces, few crimes and never dream of sex. I'll examine one of these tribes in Chapter Twenty-one.

LOVE is a higher quality than sex, arising from the same energies. Without love, sex can be just another sleeping pill for the man, who uses his wife to unload his stresses from work. To counter being used in this manner, many women get the proverbial HEADACHE, keeping the man angry and the woman lonely. This is ugly and inhuman. Sex should never be demanded or expected as is allowed by marriage.

The Indian poet, Rabindranath Tagore tells a beautiful story of a man and a woman in love. She is constantly asking him to marry her, but the man refuses. The woman asks why and he replies, "Because I love you." He finally concedes to the marriage on one condition: that they must live on opposite sides of a large lake. "Then, just by chance, as I'm walking through the garden or rowing on the lake, we'll meet, just by accident and fall in love again."

The unexpected meeting is always beautiful. Plans fail because the future is uncertain. If we can enjoy the spontaneous aspects of life, we have the key to happiness, never missing what is not possible. People go on planning, trying to control their lives and the worst possibility is that it may happen as they planned. If you know the end of the movie, why go see it?

DON'T OVER-PLAN LIFE

Life gives us so many unexpected twists and hilarious surprises. There is no better entertainment available. Seeing that LOVE is not in our hands, but comes and goes without warning, we can enjoy it when it comes and let go when it leaves.

LOVE is very fragile. It can only be held in the open hand. Try to grab it and ... POOF, gone forever. Those who claim that love is forever are only hopeful. They may carve their names in the bark of a tree, but the carving will likely outlast their love. LOVE is not PASSION. Passion is wild and feverish, while love is cool and deep. Love is the spiritual meeting of two souls, miss it and you've missed your life. Sex can enhance love, but it cannot promise love. No one can promise honestly to love another forever. Who can say what will happen in the future? Love can be invited, but not demanded. It comes like a breeze on a hot summer's day, and can stop as quickly.

When the heart is open, it transforms mundane life into bliss. Jesus hinted at the connection between the heart and the spirit when he said, "God is love." But love alone can breed possessiveness, jealousy and fear of being alone. FREEDOM is also needed so each individual can grow and change.

The greatest challenge in relating to others is how courageous you are to allow intimacy. Can you trust your lover so deeply that you can share your innermost secrets? Then you meet as friends also. Don't make promises and you'll never have to lie.

As you get closer, the need to talk constantly vanishes as your hearts begin to FEEL deeper. Communication is only a meeting of minds, but gives a bridge between two unconnected people. COMMUNION is the meeting of two hearts and talk destroys that silent electric space. Two people deeply in love tend to think the same thoughts often anyway.

A true lover can even allow his lover to move with other lovers. Just to see the one you love happy, can make you happy. Saying YES to others doesn't mean saying NO to you. If your boyfriend stops looking at other women, you can be sure, he'll stop looking at you also. If he really trusts you and your love, he may even tell you which girls he likes to look at, just as he'd tell any friend. Tell him your joys, too. Love trusts.

Love comes and goes like waves. We move close together and then we need time to be apart. If both partners understand this, they will allow each other to move away between meetings and come close when hearts are open. If love dies, there is no need to scream and demand love to return. Be grateful it had been alive, and there is every chance love will come again, especially to one who allows freedom. Remember, freedom goes two ways: freedom to go, AND freedom to come close.

CHAPTER EIGHT

... MARRIAGE?

An old man who was known as a world traveller was once asked by his young nephew, "Tell me, uncle, why is it that you never married?"

The Ancient One stroked his long white beard with a far-away look in his eyes. "I waited to meet the perfect woman. I sailed the seven seas, crossed every continent and climbed many a mountain in search of her. One day, in a crowded marketplace in Brazil, I finally found her! Her eyes sparkled like the stars at night, she could cook a meal fit only for a king and her voice was that of an angel."

"So, why didn't you marry her?" the youth asked.

"Unfortunately," the older sighed, "she was looking for the perfect man."

The perfect man, Mr. Right, your soulmate. (or is it stalemate?) They say that marriages are made in heaven. What then can be made in hell?

One middle-aged woman who had been married six times shared her wisdom with me. "I was once married to a Mormon. They believe that being married in their temple means you will live together for eternity. What a punishment that would be. I barely survived two years!"

Why is marriage hell? Why do 50% of all marriages in this country end in divorce? Do people always choose the wrong mate, or is there something wrong with the institution of marriage itself?

First of all, it's probable that the wrong mate will be chosen. Sigmund Freud points out that nuclear families create a strong bonding between the son and his mother, the daughter and her father. This makes IMPRINTS, psychological models in our heads of the right mate. But, there is no one out there exactly like your mother or father.

Take a moment to look in your local paper at the faces of newlyweds. Isn't it uncanny how many of the couples look alike? They sure look happy, don't they?

Come back in a year or two and see what's happened. That woman with the nose and hair like your mother has turned into a nagging bitch. That man who twirls his moustache like your father has transformed into Scrooge McDuck with his money, he stays out half the night drinking with the duck boys ...and the jerk snores!

When people see each other the way they really are, without the makeup and painted smiles, they often feel deceived. They cannot see that it was their own projection of PERFECTION onto the other that kept them from meeting the real person. Dreams may be lovely, but eventually you have to awaken. This poor donkey you married is not to blame.

People cling to each other even if love has died. They fear being left alone, first by parents, then by spouses. Because they were both forced to promise to love each other until death, they took each other for granted.

When two people first meet, it is out of freedom. Both are careful and gentle with each other, knowing that nothing is keeping them together but love. The beginning is always beautiful.

As the newness wears off, so does the excitement. Both lovers become aware that something has changed and may be scared of being alone again. They may both agree to marriage, saying, "Let's get serious." Have they ever looked at how much fun the serious people in the world are having: the priests, the businesspeople, the politicians?

Marriage is propounded by serious people. The churches want you to start families where the children are taught to believe their dogmas, the politicians want more voters and businesses don't want their employees distracted from work by love. A married man wants to spend more time in the office, working rather than going home to arguments. The burdens and fighting of marriage keep you interested in an afterlife.

In India, many traditional families still arrange their children's marriages, even while they are still babies. This insures that love has little chance to happen, knowing love is uncontrollable. Your daughter might fall in love with an untouchable. It is a business deal and creates many children.

Love is DANGEROUS. You cannot trust it. The heart knows no reason and can change unexpectedly. Your mind may want the love to last forever, but your heart is a true rebel. If forced to love only one person, the heart may stop loving altogether. Love is large enough to include many.

So, what to do when love has gone? Jealousy is one of the worst feelings a human can suffer. It feels as if the heart has fallen down into the stomach where it is slowly digested, or INDIGESTED. It feels as if you could die.

Jealousy is caused by a feeling of ownership, a desire to possess your lover. It is so powerful that it can destroy love without any reason, just from suspicion.

If love dies you have two choices: you can either pretend that love is still there by smiling and acting loving, or you can thank the other for the beautiful time you shared and part as friends.

The trouble with the first choice is that love cannot be cultured. Couples may stay together for decades with only the memories of the love they had and the hopes that it may come again. Those who live together after love is gone usually try to hold each other in every way, afraid to be alone. Marriage keeps couples legally bound to each other whether there is love or not.

People need FREEDOM. Without freedom, love can become a bondage. If privacy and freedom are taken away, a person must fight for it. Fighting creates distance. As soon as enough distance is created, most couples fall in love again. Distance allows them to see each other again and a desire to explore this STRANGER may arise once more. If both partners understand this, there is no need to fight any more, just allow space and the distance will invite love to blossom again and again.

In reality, we are all strangers. There is nothing more degrading to an individual than thinking you know them, with all their mysteries and depths. People are not mappable. We are all changing every day we are alive. Allowing change is the key to intimacy.

Growth is change. If we allow each other space to grow, we also get space to grow. Accepting that we are strangers keeps the mystery alive and the other person interesting. Both partners feel free to come and go, making it easy to stay. From my own experience, the only way to make it LAST is to make it NEW every moment. When you don't have to fight for your freedom, your energies can move into creativity.

Couples can evolve out of the LOVER and into the FRIEND. Friends can still be lovers, but being lovers doesn't mean you are also friends. Each should have their separate money. If the man controls the financing, there are always strings attached. Why should a grown woman have to beg for a new dress? It is part of the slavery women have suffered as possessions of men. In our culture, money equals freedom.

I am not AGAINST marriage, although it is the major cause of divorce. Anyone can get married and experiment with togetherness. It is when it becomes an addiction or co-dependency that the trouble starts. The fight for domination leads to disaster. One out of every three women in the USA gets attacked by her husband.

John Lee, my friend and author of THE FLYING BOY: HEALING THE WOUNDED MAN, runs workshops for men and women trying to break out of addictive relationships. His book details his own process of healing while his workshops explore old patterns and meetings on new levels.[4]

Marriage captures the wild bird with whom you fell in love and puts it in a cage. Do you think it's the same bird now? The magnificent eagle you loved is now a barnyard hen and you're going to get your beak pecked for caging it.

As always, it is up to you to discover if I am correct or not. I can only share my insights and experiences. At least in this country you can get a divorce. But PLEASE, don't have children until you are sure the two of you can live in harmony and love. Otherwise, you may dump all your anger on the children.

Thought of the day: Marriage is a three-ring circus: Engagement ring, Wedding ring and SUFFER-RING!

---

[4] John Lee, New Men's Press, 4204 Ave. F., Austin, TX 78751

CHAPTER NINE

SUICIDE: TO BE OR...

There seems to be a rash of teenage suicides these days. A recent newspaper article claims that since 1974, the suicide rate for teens (15-19) has made up 44% of all suicides, while all other age groups average only 2.6%. This is an important subject so turn off that rap music and tune in.

What goes on in the mind of a potential suicide victim, which could be you or me as well as anyone else? Let's listen in:

"I'll get even with them! I'm not allowed to do anything I want to do. They don't care about me. I can't live up to all their expectations. They'll be sorry when I'm dead!"

It's true, they will be sorry, but you won't even be around to dig on it. They'll probably miss you, but what good does that do for you? You've thrown away the chance to live your life the way you wanted to, and just at the time you are leaving home to go out on your own and feel your wings. Dummy!

First let me point out that EVERY intelligent person has considered suicide at one time or another. Life is not all roses. You are born with a slap on the butt, go to school for your whole childhood, work for the rest of your life and retire with a gold pocketwatch just in time to die. Why not skip the whole drag?

If that's all there is to life, I agree, but it is not! It may be all that is offered from your point of view, but who says you have to accept everything you're offered?

A close friend once confided an experience where she almost committed suicide. She was in college and struggling with the competitive environment.

"I was passing, actually doing well, but I had this ingrained fear that I was going to fail. My father always told me I would fail eventually and I'd get so shaky I couldn't even read, my mind would go blank."

Feeling like a failure, she visited a few doctors and gathered enough pills to kill herself. One night, as she sat there staring at the pills, contemplating death, a funny thing happened.

"Life seemed meaningless. As I stared at the pills, I felt powerful, as if my suicide was the one thing no one could prevent. It was my freedom and I wouldn't fail at it. I wanted my parents to feel guilty for putting so much pressure on me.

"I wondered what it would be like to be dead so I closed my eyes and tried to feel it. I fell deep inside myself and everything suddenly stopped, including time. Something blissful came over me and I couldn't remember what the problem had been. Then it dawned on me: if life is meaningless, then death is meaningless!"

She had unknowingly discovered meditation on her own, with no teacher and no ideas about it. As hard as she tried, the mysterious space would not return on her demand, but this experience began her journey toward the spiritual center of herself.

The EXISTENTIALIST movement came to the conclusion that life is meaningless, but their response was negative. They said, "If life is meaningless, why go on living?" The other side is, "If life is meaningless, why get serious? Enjoy it." This is my choice.

MEANING is an invention of MIND. It gives the ego a feeling of importance. Thousands of philosophers and religions have tried to teach people some meaning to their lives: "God wants you to spread his word, conquer the world or serve the poor. You are here to love each other or life is a test of some kind." This is how the mind creates fictions to console you so you'll feel necessary.

I'm not saying that you are not necessary. Existence has put you here right now, so you are necessary. Without you, something will be missing. What I'm saying is that you are not here for any particular PURPOSE. You are free to decide whatever you want to do. Trying to fit into some given purpose might prevent you from discovering your ultimate potentials.

Almost any day, you can read about someone who has fallen over the edge and has chosen to bite the big one. Why doesn't anyone tell this person that it's natural to fail and, "WE feel that way sometimes, too!"

INSANITY is a relative term. Being a misfit is not a sure sign of being crazy, but most likely a sign of intelligence. I don't fit in myself. I don't consider the businessman who dashes off for work in the wee hours of the morning, is tense all day, fights traffic all the way home, eats dinner, has a few drinks and hits the sack, to be truly sane. He has learned how to survive, but is he living?

There are many people who love their jobs, I'm not talking about them. It isn't what you do that matters, but the creativity and joy you bring to it. My concerns are with the people who are so scared of not surviving that they take on jobs which they hate. These people will eventually snap.

But what about YOU? You are young and haven't created too much disaster in your life yet, right? Well, not TOO much. Are you one of the sensitive individuals who cannot understand the violence and stupidities of mankind? Me too.

There are so many reasons to be unhappy in this world. You fail a test, you smash up the family car, love leaves you, your body is injured, the list is unending. Unhappiness needs a reason.

ANGUISH is a deeper version of unhappiness. The futility of life and the inability to understand who you are in a world of feuding countries armed with atomic weapons, poisoning the air, land and water ... floating on a speck of dust in an insignificant universe. Whew!

HAPPINESS is a positive thing, but very temporal. You may hit a HIGH once in a while, but it's over too soon. In the words of Ram Dass, "Will it ever be that great ice cream cone in the sky?"[5] No. Eat it or it will melt. Either way, it will be gone. ECSTASY, not the drug, is something deeper than happiness. Coming in contact with the source of life energies within you brings ecstasy. It needs no reason and it's always present once you discover the knack of going within. Then life becomes a benediction. The desire for drugs, excitement and entertainment fall away since they are not needed to cover your misery.

Sadness will still come, but you can enjoy it. All the seasons of human emotion are enjoyed if you are not identified with them, but remain watching from your ecstatic center. Ideas and emotions come and go, whatever they do is their business. You allow everything.

You don't need to kill yourself, but it is still your decision. If you are set on the idea and nothing can stop you, goodbye, I won't be hurt if you miss the next few chapters. But think first of all the chapters of your own life you'll be missing: Falling in love, painting a fabulous sunset, sipping tea on a cold winter night. If there is reincarnation, you'll be back again for the same torture of growing up. If there's one life, you've missed your only chance.

No one commits suicide who is living life with intensity and joy. If you allow others to dictate who you are supposed to be and how you are to act, then your life will be hell. It is YOUR choice.

Start writing your own script. Have fun with life, dance and celebrate. Forgive your parents or guardians for whatever nonsense they've done and whatever problems they have. Move off by yourself or with other CREATIVE REBELS who want to live their lives totally.

When there's distance, you'll be able to see your parents again and know they never meant to pressure you. Once you are taking full responsibility for your life you'll be happier and maybe you can meet them as friends.

Death is not to philosophize about. It will come for you some day and there is no need to rush it. If you have lived out everything you ever wanted to do, you can relax into death when it comes and see what it's about. Before it comes, see if you can unlock some of the mysteries of life and find the part of you that will go on.

If you are miserable, there is no need to kill yourself. Try killing the programming of your mind that has made you miserable. Be life-affirmative. Celebrate this gift.

5 Ram Dass, aka Richard Alpert, from BE HERE NOW

CHAPTER TEN

TRANSFORMING ANGER

Teenagers can expect to experience a period of extreme anger. You are not a child anymore, but you aren't accepted as an adult either. You have sexual drives which you are told not to have, you may be stuck in your parents' home and are forced to live by their rules. Most major decisions in your life are made by someone else.

Unless you are an unusually authentic (and difficult) person, there are probably times when you are false and cover up your anger. Do you smile and say, "I'm okay", even when you are burning inside? Maybe school is bumming you out because of all the useless stuff you are forced to memorize.

Constant anger is a result of not living your own life and it must be released before deep inner searching can begin. If you are in an environment where anger can be released naturally, such as chopping wood, sports or other heavy physical exercise, you are probably less prone to explosions.

With all the wild energies of youth running through your veins, it is good to channel it into something physical or you may go bananas. There are also many techniques, created by different masters, to transform anger into love, compassion and meditation. In the distant past, people were far more simple and more centered in the heart. Imagine if Jesus walked up to a fisherman today and said, "Come follow me, I'll make you a fisher of men." He'd certainly be locked in the looney-bin or arrested for conspiracy to commit kidnapping.

Modern humans have become like walking computers, processing everything with the mind instead of FEELING it. Have you ever heard someone say, "I think I'm in love." What nonsense! Love has nothing to do with thinking. The head is blocking the feelings of the heart.

The heart releases its tensions through tears. When crying is blocked, anger becomes the main release for pent-up emotions. It can be a defense to keep from feeling pain. When full, almost any little excuse can bring on violent outbursts.

Modern meditation techniques have been developed to remove anger and tension from the mind before meditating. It takes catharsis, yelling and screaming and throwing out insanity before the ancient meditation techniques can penetrate modern man.

First, select a place where you won't be disturbed, or tied into a strait jacket. Then let it fly! Be as negative as you can be for forty minutes, beat pillows, put on music that you hate, yell "NO", swear, or whatever comes out. Don't control.

Sometimes you'll laugh and be silly, other times you'll see the KILLER erupt and some innocent pillow will meet its doom. The idea is to release whatever you've been holding without involving anyone else, whom you may hurt. Since anger is often covering sadness, your FREAK IN might end in a period of tears. Your interiority will get a good scrubbing and relaxation will follow automatically. Then look into the quiet space you've just cleared.

To remain negative for the whole forty minutes is very difficult. After a short period of total rage, you'll find the anger is letting up, but you have to continue the technique for the whole period. A distance will develop between you and your anger. Anger is not you. You'll have to act angry to keep going. From that moment on, you may have this insight whenever anger bubbles up, and you won't be so identified with it.

Notice when watching rage that you are breathing in a certain manner. Repeat that same breathing when you're alone and anger will return so you can release it with this technique. Feel how your jaw gets tight, as if you are ready to bite someone. If repressed, this anger can stay in your jaw, causing grinding of the teeth during sleep or TMJ (Temporo Mandibular Joint) problems.

Yelling releases anger from the jaw. Primal scream is a therapy based in vocal expression to release tension. Crying like a baby is a lot of fun and usually ends with a good laugh. Jaw massage is also good to relax those muscles. Dumping your anger on another human being will always result in wounds. Sharing anger will create more anger. Repressing it can fill you with thorns. TRANSFORMING anger harmlessly into pure energy while you're alone solves the problem.

Another fun technique for transforming anger is to run to a mirror as soon as it starts. Look into the eyes of the killer, staring out of your own face. It is hilarious! Don't try to stop it, just observe. It is YOUR anger, the other person has simply pushed the right buttons to bring it to the surface.

Eventually, the anger will change and you may even feel deep compassion for the same person whom you were about to throw out the window only fifteen minutes before. Every extreme eventually moves to its opposite. When love comes again, that is the time to share space again.

If two people agree to help each other's spiritual growth, they will never go back to discuss an angry situation which has already passed. When both have taken full responsibility for the transformation of their own anger, two new people are meeting, as if for the first time. Anger was a storm which came and went and this fresh moment must be unhindered by the past. This WORKS!

Most people try to WORK OUT problems, causing egos to clash and both get pulled back into the confrontation. Let the past be past. The mind is not the right place to meet again, only hearts can meet.

People often have short fuses because they are sitting on a volcano of repressions. One wrong step and KA-POW! It is far better to remove the nitroglycerin with fun techniques than to wait for it to blow. The nicest guy is often the one who explodes and kills himself and others in a rage.

Since the focus of spiritual evolution is in bringing awareness to everything, anger becomes a great opportunity to transform a large amount of energy into positive growth. Notice how easy it is to start anger but, after it kicks in, it goes beyond your control. The brain releases chemicals and the body takes over. It is only your choice in the very beginning.

Try this one: As soon as you realize you are sliding into an old pattern of outrage, close your eyes and bring in AWARENESS. Without repressing or expressing, anger is transformed, melting before the flame of awareness.

Only someone with the capacity to get explosively angry can also have the ability to love deeply. It is a question of energy. By holding anger, you hold back all energies. In the release of blocked emotions, you free the very energies that can flower in you as bliss and creativity. LOVE is expansive enough to contain a hint of anger. A parent who never gets angry shows a lack of caring. In a way, a blast of anger helps a child to know he is loved, and is now forgiven for the mistake. He has paid the price and is even with the world. Otherwise, guilt feelings may remain, stuffed in the subconscious.

For about a year, my friend Mati and I decided to call each other disgusting names, just to reach the point where we could laugh instead of getting hurt by insults. We came up with some real kickers and most people thought we were fighting. The techniques worked and we are now almost unaffected by verbal attack.

After doing purging techniques for a while to cut the deep roots of anger, we return to a natural relaxed state where anger-flares are momentary. Without roots, even a short blast of anger will not be unnecessarily vicious, making love infinitely stronger.

So, first dump out your toxic hates, and then soft techniques like watching your breath come in and go out will have a deepening effect. Life and death are meeting in you with every breath, and awareness of this will expand slowly into every cell of your body. Otherwise, sitting silently, looking in, you may find yourself face-to-face with the dragon.

CHAPTER ELEVEN

DROPPING OUT

A common question I hear from teenagers is, "Why should I stay in school when I'm not learning anything valuable?" I can understand the question. If teachers are boring you can't even hear what they are saying. Schools teach us to be competitive, to struggle to WIN. This naturally means that someone else is going to LOSE. Grades are often marked on a CURVE, meaning someone will always pass and someone is doomed to fail! Even the ones who succeed will feel tremendous pressure to keep on top. I once watched an A+ student get her first B. She almost had a nervous breakdown right there in the fourth grade.

Many children grow up with a LOSER image which they learned in school, maybe only because they don't have a good memory. Intelligence is not memory. They originate in two separate parts of the brain. Even Albert Einstein was a deplorable student.

Realizing this fact, many European schools have begun to give exams in the library, allowing students to bring textbooks and research tests. The questions are never known in advance. The results showed that the normal "A" students began to fail and usually poor students often became the best. It takes intelligence to find information and good memories are not enough.

With competition and judgment, there will always be jealousy. Once a child is bribed with rewards for success in classes, he will do anything to win. The family ego wants their child to be the best. The WINNER often sucks up to the teacher in hopes of getting special attention while the LOSER is filled with self condemnation and anger.

An ancient Zen story tells of a Samurai warrior who goes to visit a Zen Master. Just coming in contact with the Master, the Samurai begins to feel inferior. He asks the Master why. The Master leads him into the garden and shows him the bushes and trees, all living next to each other in harmony. "Do you think the bush asks why it is not a large tree?" asks the Master. "The rose is not trying to become a daisy. It is content to be what it is." The Samurai understood and never compared himself to others again.

Because of competition, people get so afraid of failure that they never try anything new. Later in life they may even choose a job they hate just to impress their parents and get respect of their peers. They remain miserable. What a waste of life.

All of us make mistakes, but that doesn't mean we are losers. Instead of trying to be perfect, be TOTAL. Try whatever is new and see if it works. If not, try something else. This is learning. Just don't keep making the same mistakes again.

I've never seen a public school that is interested in helping you discover who you really are. Instead, they try to mold you into someone they would like you to become. No one is interested in what you want. Who is there to guide you toward your dreams and potentials?

When I was in high school, I earned many awards. Each time I would receive one, I got a temporary ego rush. People would clap and make me feel I had done something great, then they would forget about me. For one brief moment, I was accepted, but the adrenaline would soon wear off and I would be nobody special again.

This was my first experience with the fact that success can't make you happy. It is a tease. After each success, you have to pick a new goal and try to win again. I decided that there must be something else, something lasting and began my quest.

School can be a sort of jail, but only if you interpret it in that way. Dreaming about being somewhere else and doing something else can't change where you ARE. If you are forced to be in school, you might as well have a good time with it and get something positive out of it.

So, if you're in school, how can you transform the classroom into something interesting and beneficial? You can't be forced to believe and parrot everything you're told. Ask the teachers to PROVE what they are teaching, what is their source? Have they explained it well enough that you can understand it and why do they consider it significant for you to know this.

Ask your teachers how much of what they teach is from their own experiences, or did it just come from a book or another teacher? By questioning FACTS, you'll find out more about reality and sharpen your intelligence at the same time. Always DOUBT until proof is offered and you can never be exploited with lies.

Bad teachers can become very disturbed by intelligent questions, especially if they don't know the answers. You'll quickly learn which teachers are honest and can admit that there are things they don't know. It gives them a chance to do research with you. Other teachers will have so much ego that they can't admit ignorance and may even lie to the class.

A REBEL may be labelled as a trouble-maker, but the focus is not on creating trouble, but finding TRUTH. You didn't choose to come to school, you are forced to come. Not wanting to waste time learning lies and half-truths, you inspire the teachers to go beyond the boring textbooks.

This will transform the classroom into a place to sharpen intelligence instead of regurgitate FACTS. All the students will begin to question and listen more instead of daydreaming to escape from the boredom. An honest and sincere teacher will welcome your questions and enthusiasm and will guide you to the answers to all your questions.

I was lucky enough to have an English teacher in high school who inspired the whole class to new heights of creative writing. She issued us each a blank book and suggested we write four entries per week. It could be a short story, a poem, thoughts or even a limerick. The class caught fire and the pieces she read aloud were amazing.

Since I was already interested in the environment, I wrote a piece about pollution and how we all add to the problem by accepting extra packaging, supporting factories which pollute and by not recycling. The surprise was that the entire work was written backward and I intentionally scribbled all over the other side so she couldn't hold it up to a light, and would probably seek a mirror.

The last line read, "You are as guilty as everyone else for this catastrophe., how can you look at yourself in this mirror?" She told me she freaked out, looking around to see if I had followed her home and was watching her with the mirror.

My point is that her enthusiasm and support for our efforts enhanced our individuality and we rose to the task. I wonder how many of my classmates also became writers. Good teachers can and do inspire students.

School should be a jumping board for the rest of life. Do you plan to spend all your life memorizing which idiot attacked what country in which year? Most likely, your life will be a quest, a seeking into the mysteries of life, a journey toward truth and love. What better time to get started than in school?

Take the challenge. If school is HELL, you are partly to blame. Do you just sit there like a corpse, waiting for the poor teacher to entertain you? The energies of youth are overflowing and you are only doing what you need to pass. Get off your butt and make it interesting, develop your potentials.

Since you are allowed to drop out at a certain age, each individual has to make that decision. One consideration must be, do you want to get a job someday? It's almost impossible to get a job without a high school education. If you've already dropped out, and are able to read this book, get your GED. It's not that hard and it gives you job freedoms of other high school graduates.

If you are planning a career which demands special training, it might be wise to take a year off and travel a bit before going into college. You may not ever get the chance again.

A good friend of mine decided to become a lawyer. She had to borrow a small fortune to go to law school and it had to be paid back, starting immediately after graduation. I ran into her after law school and she said, "I'm not sure I want to be a lawyer now." It was too late. She went straight to work and has worked ever since. Now it has been eighteen years since she graduated from high school and she still hasn't taken time to travel.

School can be a valuable stairway to success in the world, but success cannot give you inner peace. There has to be a balance. Dropping out completely will mean POVERTY and climbing the corporate ladder will take your whole life away.

A distant relative of mine barely finished high school, with her grades right on the borderline. People thought she was unintelligent, but she was bored, dreaming of all the freedom she'd have when she finally got out of school. After high school, she tried everything she'd been dreaming about and found it wasn't as much fun as she thought. She returned to school, took all the classes which interested her, got excellent grades and became a teacher. Then everyone was proud of her. Soon it became apparent that teaching couldn't make her happy either and she turned to alcohol. She had finally made it in the world, and had become as miserable as everyone else.

My point here is that school is an OUTWARD tool which aids your living in the world, but it can't satisfy your yearning to know yourself. You'll need to work to make money to live on, but choose a job you like and make sure you get equal time for falling in love, meditation and outdoor activities. Outer and inner riches can come together.

The entire WORLD is a school and we're all teachers and students. Everyone we meet shows us something about ourselves, but are we really learning? The 90s are decisive, learn how to live together or the school may be out FOREVER.

DON'T LET SCHOOLS BECOME FACTORIES

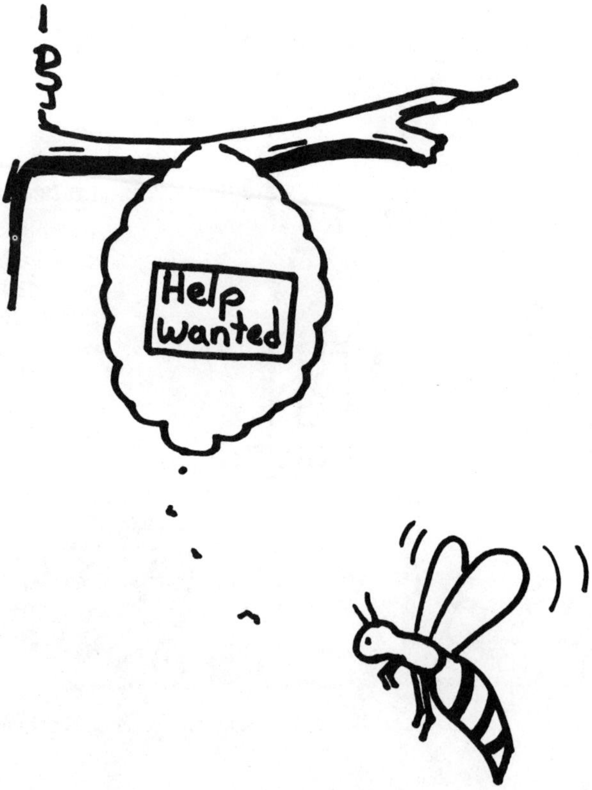
Help wanted

CHAPTER TWELVE

DOES IT WORK?

When I was just leaving high school and setting off for college, people asked me repeatedly, "What are you going to major in?" I imagine it was a relevant question to the ones who asked, but it sounded to me like, "What prison are you narrowing yourself to?"

I managed to go the whole four years without deciding and graduated with a BA in "Selected Studies". There was nothing to decide. I was going to study anything I was interested in and I had no desire to BECOME anybody. I studied everything from Edible Plants of the Rocky Mountains, and Folk-medicines, to Women's Liberation and Psychology.

I never wanted to have a career. The very idea of doing one thing for the rest of my life was absurd. I would do whatever job I felt like doing as long as it allowed me to survive. After college, I bought an old condemned house in Alamosa, Colorado for $3,000! I put down one-thousand I'd made fighting forest fires and paid one hundred dollars per month for two years.

So far, I've worked as a swimming instructor and lifeguard, driver for handicapped people, school bus driver, cook, waiter, dishwasher, forest fire fighter, house painter, clerk, metaphysical bookstore manager, beadworker, apple harvester, juice bar owner, solar unit builder, mushroom harvester, fire wood hauler, owner of a business to remove parasites from trees, psychic healer, college lecturer, musician, painted tee-shirts, movie extra and now I'm writing and making fuzzy puppets for children. Who knows what I'll do tomorrow?

To most people, their jobs have become part of their egos, providing them with a sense of USEFULNESS. In a competitive atmosphere, some jobs are considered to be superior to others. Why does a business executive feel superior to the man who sweeps his office? Both are needed. The sweeper may even have more fun and is under a lot less stress.

I deeply appreciated reading Henry David Thoreau in college. He noted that it takes only a couple of hours per day to gather the ESSENTIALS for life and the remainder of the day is freed for whatever creative activities you choose to do. He was studying Walden Pond, feeling that it was a Microcosm of the whole existence. He hypothesized that understanding a small piece of existence would bring understanding of the Macrocosm, the entire existence. I spent a whole winter fixing up the little house without working a regular job. Many times, I came down to my last five dollars and decided to buy some delicious dessert. My girlfriend at the time usually freaked out. She was working and made it clear that she would not support me, but I was equally clear that I had to spend the last money to make a vacuum. Nature abhors vacuums and new money would have to come to fill the space. It always came.

I couldn't count the number of times money has come to me, just in time to pay the bills. But I was not trying to MANIFEST anything. It was a matter of TRUST. The house needed fixing so I did it. Food was needed and it came. A two-day job would be offered just as the money was gone, and I always said YES. I still do.

It is useless to go beating on closed doors trying to force whatever you envisioned should happen. If you are AVAILABLE to the present moment, existence shows you which doors are open. There is no need to choose; the best option is obvious if you look without preconceived ideas.

Even losing a job can be a lot of fun. My priorities have always been to follow my heart and that often put me at odds with my BOSS. One time, I was fired for refusing to drive a school bus which I knew had bad brakes. After consistently bringing it to the attention of my supervisor, who was also the mechanic, I refused to drive until the bus was fixed. The boss knew he couldn't fire me under those circumstances.

He gave me a two day break on my birthday and hired someone else while I was gone, claiming I hadn't shown up for work in two days without permission. It could have been a major drag for someone else, but I figured it was time to move on to something new and found work which was more fun to do in a few weeks.

I tried every angle of the restaurant business, starting with cooking. For $3.25 per hour, I found myself running a sixteen burner stove, three microwaves, two ovens and a sandwich board by myself; cooking for the whole restaurant. I hadn't any experience, but jobs were tough at the time and I learned fast. The owner of the restaurant used to test me by coming in to order an omelet, his favorite meal, right at the peak of the rush hour. This idiot would stand behind me and watch each move to see if I could keep up with twenty orders, plus his stupid omelet, which had to be perfect.

On one occasion, when I was in training, I was left alone to cook for the entire restaurant and there was no prep-cook on the line to help. I'm a vegetarian and was just learning how to cook meats. There had been many orders for beef Stroganoff that night and the white sauce used for the gravy ran out. Of course, one more order for beef Stroganoff came in. Now what to do? I had no time to look through the cook books and find out exactly what went into the white sauce, and no time to spare for making it if I'd known how. It was time for creativity! As I tossed in the meat to brown, I scanned the place for a possible substitute. The Au Jus sauce would be a good broth, but it had to be white. I tossed in a glop of yogurt and a splash of sour cream, selected some green spices and tossed the steaming concoction over the noodles.

It looked pretty real and I thought I'd get away with it. Half an hour later, one of the waitresses came to find me. "You know that last Stroganoff you made?" I nodded sheepishly. "The man said to give you his compliments. It was the best Stroganoff he'd ever tasted in his life."

When I lived in Denver, I took on a job as a waiter in a fancy restaurant in the Cherry Creek area. It was a hassle to memorize everything on the menu and what was in it, including forty wines, but I managed in a week. For some reason, the Big Cheese chose me as his WHIPPING BOY. He'd follow me around and talk to me right in the middle of serving six tables, filled with people who'd asked me for something or other.

Many a night, I'd come home exhausted from the pressure and angry at the little rat for keeping me distracted. Finally, one day, he came in with a chip on his shoulder larger than his brain and fired me for missing a salad dressing. A great feeling of relief came over me. "I'm fired?" I asked happily. He nodded. "Great!" I said. "Then I don't have to put up with your constant interference. You are like an angry Chihuahua, barking at me all day..."

I really gave it to him. To my surprise, he stood there with his mouth open, thanked me for telling him how I felt, and rehired me. He never bothered me again. I learned to communicate my feelings directly and honestly.

Loving the great outdoors and the strength I feel from heavy physical labor, I began fighting forest fires. At the time, I was a long-hair in looks, and a health food nut in foods. This was quite a clash with the redneck Montana boys who formed the Helena Interagency Hotshot Crew. They found it great fun to torture me. I didn't try in any way to fit in. I enjoyed rock music instead of country, wore one earring, and worst of all ... I didn't drink beer! It was a long summer.

Before the next fire season started, I had begun meditating, met my spiritual guide, Osho, and found a new life within. I returned the next summer wearing bright red clothing and a beaded necklace. They took one look at me and knew I'd flipped my tofu burger. It was an amazing change. They all enjoyed me as a character and no one was hostile anymore. I loved the work and volunteered for every job offered, setting a new record for line-digging in a government study and I never seemed to run out of energy.

Sometimes the fire overtook us and we were told to withdraw, but I was always the last to go. I loved watching the two-hundred foot flames rushing up the hill at us, the sky darkened except a red dot where the sun was, and the roar of the flames as if a jet plane was crashing. It was powerful and dangerous and made me feel more alive.

Because I had become less serious and more filled with energy, I was given excellent recommendations from that fire season. By dumping all the moral trips in my head and having a drink of beer with the boys, they could see me as a person and I became friends with them all.

My own experience with jobs is that they come when you need them. I trust life. Whatever it brings is acceptable to me. One time, it gave me a broken back when my van was rear-ended. That was when I started writing. It was obviously not the time to fight forest fires any more, so it seemed appropriate to write. Life is only a problem if you can't accept it.

There is little chance of making big bucks as a teenager, working for only minimum wage or less. This makes drug dealing and other scams tempting because of the big bucks, but it may ruin your life forever. Drug dealers get shot, ripped off, and busted. They get so addicted to the lifestyle and the money that they may never be able to work again.

The job market is competitive and aggressive. Bosses can play power games on you, especially if you are a minority or a woman. Sexual harassment is forbidden by law, but hard to prove. This gives you a choice. Either you can become obsessed with the rewards of success like everyone else and start stepping on others to get ahead, or you can choose not to play such an idiotic game. What else can you do?

Programs are being set up in large cities to help young people start their own businesses. This is a great idea. You won't have a boss to put up with, you decide your hours and how much energy you want to put into it, and you learn how to survive with your own intelligence and creativity. Small business courses are offered at most colleges as mini-courses and can show you how to set up and keep your books correctly.

In owning your own business, however small, you may struggle a bit more than having a regular paycheck each week, but you'll never have to be abused by some angry boss. If you make enough to live on, that's all that's needed. You don't have to become rich, just survive. If you are doing what you enjoy the most, you'll put more love and care into it and who knows?...maybe you WILL become wealthy.

Henry Ford was once asked how he became so rich. He replied, "I've never missed an opportunity!" That's the trick. You don't have to MANIPULATE reality. Some doors open, others close. Just be ready to change as life changes and choose the door that's open. Henry Ford also admitted that he fought his way up the corporate ladder and reached the top, but found there was nothing there. He felt stupid, wasting his life to become rich instead of relaxing sometimes and enjoying life.

If you have no idea what it is you are going to do next, you can't fail. Whatever it is you do is the next step of your life. Being fired can get you moving into a better position than the old job. Don't JUDGE life. Who knows what you will be doing next? What a blessing not to be working for someone who doesn't like you or appreciate your efforts anymore.

MAKE SURE YOUR JOB FITS YOU

I've always had a hard time working for someone else because I don't recognize HIERARCHY. I have no interest in being a boss, nor do I want some dominating idiot to tell me what to do all the time. Therefore, I usually choose jobs where I am free to be creative and to be outdoors. For the last few years, I've worked only for myself, or for someone who allows me my creative space.

Just the idea of WORK has a negative connotation to it. It seems to indicate struggle. Coming in contact with my own life energies, I feel that everything I do has become PLAY. Bringing fun into work transforms every job into a playful experience. The work you perform can be the same as everyone else's, but the quality of expressiveness you pour into it adds a new dimension to the doing. The result is usually far better when you have fun with your creation.

In choosing a job, it's important that your heart is into your work. If you really care about the QUALITY of life on our planet, it will be impossible to work for the nuclear industry or something else that pollutes or kills.

Another friend of mine joined the army, knowing they would help pay for his college expenses. During his training period, I visited him and I could hardly believe the change. He was more fit than I'd ever seen him and his self-confidence was at a new high, but he was anxious to go to Vietnam to kill Gooks! I was astounded. He was never prejudiced before, the guy was white and had a black girlfriend. Now, looking back, he can't believe it either. He had been BRAINWASHED into hatred.

A man who is in his heart cannot be a killer. What intelligent person will turn right, then turn left on command? It is a training so you will kill when ordered to. The army may be a great place to burn off some anger, but what is the cost?

Kids who've had no power in their lives are given automatic weapons and sent into some faraway country to fight for oil companies. Is that really "All that you can be?"

The main lure for joining the armed forces is to gain skills which can be used in later life, even though statistics compiled by the Veterans Education Project show that only 12% of those leaving the military have acquired skills applicable to civilian life. What is it we are told we must fight for? FREEDOM! What freedom does a young man have who gets drafted into the army, goes to war and dies? Another man may come home to find he cannot fit into the society again and he may wind up living on the streets, unemployable.

The Gulf War was more of a massacre than a war. Many young people may be thinking that war is always quick and easy and the good guys always win. We see parades costing twelve million dollars to celebrate the murder of a hundred thousand people, because they were enemies. Certainly, the troops who went to the Mid East and fought were brave, well-trained and deserve love and acceptance upon their return, but did they really need to go in the first place?

If you are interested in hearing about the other side of war, contact the VETERANS EDUCATION PROJECT at PO Box 416, Amherst, MA 01004. They will send ex-military people to your school to tell you about the physical, psychological and social scars war leaves behind. It will be an experience you'll never forget.

Because of poverty, lack of schooling or various other reasons, many minority teens join the armed forces. As we have seen in the Persian Gulf, war can happen at any moment and you may be forced to kill or be killed. The numbers of Blacks and Hispanics fighting is disproportional to the amount of whites, who may find better jobs.

Recently, though, minorities have begun their own businesses and developed a name for themselves for their good work. As the business grows, more friends can join. Look at M.C. Hammer. He seems to have hired all his relatives and friends to dance, and share in his success.

To start out, you might find other CREATIVE REBELS who want to go into business with you. Start with something that doesn't take a lot of money to start, like painting tee shirts, doing a show or something people might pay to see. If you live together and split the rent, you can all survive quite well.

Whenever you invent something new, it'll take time for it to catch on. It may be wiser to create a new improved version of something that is already in demand. If your creation doesn't sell at first, don't worry. Existence needs a bit of persuasion before spending a lot of energy on something new. Statistics report that only 3% of the sales on a new product go to the inventor.

After the car accident in which my back was broken, I decided never to waste a moment of my life doing something I don't want to do. When death comes, I'll be able to relax and see what death is all about. Most people seem to fight for more life because there are so many things they haven't done yet, so much life they never lived. With each sentence I write, I am finished again. If death strikes me in the middle of a sentence ... cough, ...ugh....... finished.......
It adds a bit of mystery, don't you think?

But you don't need to have a car wreck to decide to live your own life. Just choose a basic direction, something creative you've always thought of doing, and have the guts to jump into it. The funny thing is, the more risks I've taken, the more beauty existence has showered on me.

So many people who see my partner, Mati, who's making beautiful sweaters, and me owning our own businesses, designing and creating all day, say to us, "Wow! I wish I had the talent to do something creative like that. I envy you guys."

Our only answer is, "We just never learned that we couldn't "

CHAPTER THIRTEEN
POLI-TRICKS

THE WORST DRUGS

When I entered college, I found that most of the American History I had been taught up to that time was propaganda, meant to instill nationalism in the students. For example, I was horrified to see how the American Indian was abused and massacred in the name of "Manifest Destiny", meaning that America was bound to expand and no one is responsible for the inevitable clash of the cultures. The government repeatedly lied to the Indians, murdered them, starved them, even spread small pox on purpose through the villages.

When I first found out about this, in the land of the free, I was very angry. Many events of history have been changed in the books to fit the ideals supposedly sacred in this country, which we hear is only done in Russia. We now see our government carrying out plots to overthrow other governments with covert operations, as in Nicaragua. We attack Iraq for their "naked aggression", totally forgetting that is how we built our country, fighting Indians, English, French, Spanish and Mexicans.

There is no need to harp on the crimes and the lies, but we need to come back into line with the principles of Justice and Freedom promised to all by the Bill of Rights. You will be the next generation to take on this immense responsibility, and you will have to decide how your world should be run and whom you will support in government.

For this reason, you should remain well-informed about the world situation, which is changing every day. Up until now, most countries in the world are spending much of their budget, four million dollars every ten minutes, on weaponry. All this money could easily have wiped out hunger and most diseases in the entire world, if it had gone into creative projects.

We have seen a turnabout in world politics as Gorbachev has opened the doors to democracy in his country, sparking a worldwide demand for freedom. Despite the violent crushing of the freedom movement in China, most of these protests are becoming successful as we see in almost every Soviet-block nation.

Then another outside enemy appears, in the Middle East. The armies of the world have backed the United Nations for the first time. Still, few have questioned the need for controlling oil interests instead of developing alternative sources of energy, like non-polluting hydrogen. Most inventions which replace the need for gasoline have been blocked by the oil companies because of the revenues the oil companies would lose. That huge international army could be cleaning up the environment.

Up until now, each country has tried to instill a feeling of national, racial or religious pride in their countrymen. You are an American, Russian, Black, White, Catholic or Muslim. This mass ego is indoctrinated into the children of every country, even the most poor and backward, that their country is the best on Earth. But it is one Earth! Why the need for competition again? We can all live in freedom and shared wealth.

Anything done in one country affects all the other countries. The destroying of the rain forests in Brazil speeds up the greenhouse effect. The cutting of trees in Nepal causes the disastrous floods in Bangladesh. But Nepal is poor and selling the trees allows them to survive a bit longer.

A WORLD GOVERNMENT could make sure that each country has the ability to survive and work out the problems on a global level. This may be a radical approach to the mess we're in, but it's time for something radical to be done. Totally rad!

It seems that politicians, who keep most of our money tied up in DEFENSE, are not keen on the idea of a world government. By keeping their people afraid of some declared enemies, they can pour money into weaponry, and they can keep their positions as leaders. For many years, people have voted for politicians who will keep jobs available, even if the jobs were concerned with death and nothing else. As you get old enough to vote, you have to weigh your own priorities and see what kind of world you want to live in. If the same money that is spent on DEATH was put into ECOLOGY and science to heal our ailing planet, there would still be just as many jobs, but with a new focus. Shared wealth is possible and there need not be homeless people, hungry people, or ill people on the Earth. Our government even pays farmers not to grow food, so the food prices will stay high. Why not grow the food and send it to the hungry for the same cost?

Organized religions, which are very strong in politics, are also threatened by the concept of one world. As the population has grown and better transportation and communication have been developed, members of different religions meet and interact with members of other belief systems. It doesn't require too much intelligence to see that the religious teachings of each group vary geographically. But what does TRUTH have to do with geography? Doubts arise as to who, if anybody, believes the right thing. Beliefs only hide ignorance.

Churches have always killed or tortured non-believers and kept their FLOCK from mixing with others, but this has become impossible. We are living in a golden time of history, where religious indoctrination is no longer necessary. In the past, the masses may have been civilized and controlled with religious doctrines and the fear of divine punishment, but now comes the time of INDIVIDUAL RELIGIOUS EXPERIENCE.

The organized religions have forbidden birth control in an effort to make more converts to their religion. With the world almost drowning in people, we've reached a point where birth control is a NECESSITY for survival. As our focus turns toward quality of life instead of quantity, religions will have to bend their rules, or be disbanded.

Nostradamus, the sixteenth-century seer, told of a fork in the road we are now coming to. Either we will all perish in a nuclear disaster, or a thousand years of peace will come. In his recent work, NOSTRADAMUS AND THE MILLENNIUM, author John Hogue examines many of the correct forecasts of Nostradamus in the past, and offers possibilities for our future. It is, according to this source, totally up to us which road we choose!

It takes only one idiot to start World War III, and there must be thousands of idiots out there, but that is no reason to get depressed and angry. We have NOW, and that is the only time there is. Instead of fighting, celebrate life!

Whether it affects the world around you or not, reaching the blissful peaks of your consciousness makes the whole experience here worthwhile. Your blossoming as an individual WILL affect the world around you, but that can't be the focus. It is a by-product of your flowering. Just this moment, listen to the birds out there. Hear the wind. Feel your breath pulling in new life, and blowing out the dead air. Existence is flowing through every cell of your body. Can you feel it?

If you treat this moment as the only reality, you can enjoy moving in a positive direction, not worrying if you'll reach anywhere or not. Having no ideas of where you will be next, you can't lose. Wherever you are is the goal. The going is the reward itself. How CREATIVE can you get with this insight?

Conflict in the outside world usually has roots in the inner world. By eliminating conflict in yourself, you have made a proper step toward world peace. Trying to change the world is an excellent way to miss yourself; it is a big place. But transforming yourself to reach your highest potential of ecstasy and intelligence, will certainly invite the rest of the world to do the same. Many people living in freedom and love can turn the whole world around. Just look, it CAN happen!!

Young people are usually more optimistic and anxious to try something new and positive. Older people have more economic and emotional investment in the work-a-day society of the past and its rules. The past has to GO. It is what has led us to the brink of total annihilation.

Guns are for cowards and bombs are for even bigger cowards. Killing someone from a distance without having to even see their faces is totally inhuman. It only shows how unsure nations are of their ways of life. If their ways are so great, why doesn't everyone see it? People need to communicate on a GLOBAL level.

The youth of today will have to be prepared to live in a new and loving way, without repeating the mistakes of the past. This will pave the way to a bright new future.

While you're young, it's a great idea to travel and see different parts of the world. There are many special offers for teenagers, such as the Euro-rail train system in Europe. You buy one ticket and use it for a month or so. It is not offered to older folk. To meet people in other lands is the best way to see that we are all pretty much alike, but different enough to keep it interesting. Visiting foreign lands and people of other races is extremely educational, especially if your parents have chosen a particular group of people to hate. Meet the GLOBAL COMMUNITY.

Seeing how the masses in other countries have been programmed into beliefs and customs can help you to understand your own conditioning. An old Sufi saying goes, "It is easier to see a speck of dust in your friend's eye than to see an entire camel in your own eye." Just watching the accepted behavior and ideas of a large group of people can give you infinite insight into your own set of ideas about reality.

Many countries and cultures differ on subjects such as religion, afterlife, interactions between men and women, homosexuality, proper diet, morals, etc. They have accepted the way they've been taught is the right way, just as you have been taught according to the culture you were born into.

In India, a man and woman cannot show any affection to each other in public. On the same street, a man might gouge holes in his arms as a religious offering and many people will touch his feet and think he is great. For some strange reason, people are impressed by masochism and feel it is something holy.

Most of what is seen in India on the streets would bring out the police here, just as holding hands or kissing in public would bring out the police there. Every country and religion has a different morality to which members are expected to adhere.

Because of the small planet we are living on, which gets smaller every day, many cultures are facing a loss of their past. Minority groups are constantly crying that the young are not following the old ways, but are moving away, maybe to the cities.

Indian reservations are seeing fewer young members following the traditional ways and even learning the original language of the tribe. From my perspective, old languages were simply ways that people learned to communicate when they were isolated from other groups. Now the world is in full communication between all its people and dead languages can only keep us separated.

Since the English colonized much of the Earth and people speak English in most countries as the official business language, I foresee it as the easiest universal language.

So, why then should anyone be concerned with the old trad- itions, many of which are based in superstition and outdated ideologies? How can we pour an individual human being into a mold and try to make him fit into a worn-out path? There is a subtle reason why people try.

By making someone fulfill a set of characteristics, cultures reward him with a sense of fitting in, of being accepted. This ego makes the alone individual feel identified with his culture, that he knows who he is. But no individual is the PAST of a group of people. Each being is a new start, absolutely unique. The past has been filled with cruelty, imperialism, greed, murder, and insanity. At least let the new flower grow in virgin soil.

It's fine to have books in which you can read about all the cultures that ever lived here, but just take what is beneficial to you. Every culture has its dark points, and the good and bad come together. There is no need to be proud because your ancestors came from Italy or Scotland. Why should you feel superior if you are an American or a Russian? Who cares if your parents were Catholic or Islamic? Why add skin color to our differences?

We are all ordinary people, ORDINARILY SPECIAL. Other groups are not responsible for our problems. We are. Hatred is self-defeating. It will eat you from the inside. Love brings understanding, but it's up to you to allow it.

Politicians may well be the most psychologically sick people in the world. Whatever the crowd wants, the politician has to run around to the front of the group and act as if he's leading. Just for the fame and recognition, the poor fellow has to become a prostitute, selling whatever the voters want.

A REBEL cannot be part of a crowd. Wherever he stands, he is absolutely alone, whether there is a crowd around him or not. His actions will come from his consciousness, not from the acceptance of the crowd. Still, there is no need to confront and be murdered by an angry mob unless you are finished with your life. Crowds are not interested in truth. They are comfortable with consoling lies, and will gladly murder you if you create doubt. History is filled with the persecution of truth.

Remember that NEWS is created by newspeople. Don't believe everything you hear or read. The masses may be fooled by media censorship, but real individuals check sources and aren't so easily swayed for or against anyone.

History as presented may or may not be true. The present is the only time we can know and it is still unwritten. You can write whatever you wish. Things will continue to happen beyond your control, but your response becomes your personal dance with the universe. There is no need to control it, life happens. It's like playing a constant pin-ball game, you respond quickly and spontaneously as life unfolds. Enjoy living now. Who knows if you'll get ANOTHER game?

CHAPTER FIFTEEN

POWER
THROUGH THE PEEP-HOLE

Power basically means HAVING ABILITY, but it has evolved into many other meanings, including THE ABILITY TO CONTROL OTHERS. Who, in his right mind, would want to control others? No one. Only those in a wrong mind want power over others.

From a spiritual standpoint, MIND is the cause of all suffering. It is the mind which carries memories of injustice, ideas of inferiority and superiority, and divides the world into dichotomies. Therefore, even to say RIGHT mind is not descriptively correct. Being stuck in the mind clouds the vision of reality and causes us to create hierarchies and other power trips.

The quest for power is a road of suffering. Who is interested in power? Only someone who feels inferior and weak. Those who've been subservient want powerful positions to establish their domination, in an attempt to heal their feelings of inferiority by controlling others. It becomes a sort of fever, trying to dominate more people so they can feel significant.

It has been said that power corrupts, but it seems that the corruption comes long before the will-to-power. It is very easy to create inferiority feelings in children, even by accident. A child is so helpless, having to depend on the parents or authority figures for everything. There is little chance of SELF DETERMINATION for children, and children know it.

The trouble starts when parents start putting conditions on their acceptance. No society yet seems to be able to love its children just because they are alive; it always demands some kind of remuneration. The child feels like a TEAM member who is expected to succeed to be accepted by the family, or the community.

Parents are not only in a position to control general behavior, but to control what time to eat, what time to sleep, what to wear and a thousand other rules. Is there any wonder we have all lost touch with our natures when everything natural has been forced to fit into an imposed schedule?

Most intelligent children rebel naturally against this politics at an early age. It is the birth of refusal, once again, the power of NO. The parents are so strong, it is useless to try to fight them, but children can refuse to obey.

When a child gets hungry, it is the RIGHT time to eat. Why should a child have to wait for "suppertime"? Why should a playful child be sent to bed when he isn't tired? Going to bed becomes a punishment in the minds of the young when it should be considered a blissful reward after a busy and creative day.

Parents who rule with an iron hand show no respect for the integrity of their children. The child will learn to be quiet and polite to avoid being constantly punished, but he will become a hypocrite. Deep inside, the cultured child is ready to explode, but it might not be until he reaches teen-age before he blows up.

A child who doesn't obey is often punished for challenging the power of the parents. They can rationalize that "It was for her own good" or "He makes his own punishments by the way he acts," but really, it is because the parents' ego has been challenged. If the act was wrong, the child will see the damage it has caused without the parental thrashing.

Children outgrow being children, legally in eighteen years, but parents never seem to outgrow being parents. Even when they are married and have moved away from home, offspring are still bombarded with well-intentioned advice and manipulative suggestions in the name of RESPECT. If respect needs to be demanded, it is usually unwarranted.

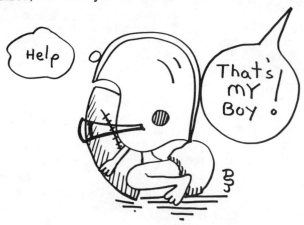

The Latin root of respect is RESPECTUS meaning LOOKING AT. By that definition, a respectful person is one who can look at anybody, even a small child, and really see them as human beings, not subservient little puppets.

It is difficult to put yourself into the shoes of another and see what he is feeling, but it is the only way to understand him. Few teenagers realize the pain and suffering they put their parents through in the name of freedom, and parents often forget what it was like to be young and restless.

I agree that only an idiot will always behave the way he is told to without questioning and that "doing your own thing" is the first step in the evolution of your individuality, but there is no need to intentionally cause heart attacks. Also, parents have to ask themselves if their rules are really for the good of their children, or merely to maintain domination.

There is one freedom in life which I consider to be the most important: the right to be alone. PRIVACY is important to mental health; just a space to be with yourself and to look into your being is absolutely necessary. Even looking at a person who wishes to be alone is an interference, disrespectful.

Although parents have the POWER to control their children in many ways, and disturbing their privacy is only one aspect of it, the parents must realize that they are creating a distance between themselves and their kids. A parent who respects his child as an equal human being, only younger, will offer the freedom to be alone, and to learn by mistakes.

If the parents don't care about the child and ignore whatever he is doing, it can be just as bad. So many children turn angry because love has been missing in their lives. Therefore, a parent has the power to overly control and the power to ignore a child, both to disastrous ends. A balance is needed.

Those who've missed love and doubt their own self-worth are doomed to seek power over others. All the politicians, generals, foremen, etc. have a need to feel necessary. The more the hurt inside, the greater the need to be a LEADER

Fortunately, there are not enough positions in politics and religions for all the hurt people in the world, or we would probably have destroyed the entire Earth by now. Millions of people who've picked up inferiority feelings from schools and homes try to find their own little ways of dominating.

Even the seemingly powerless job of a clerk becomes a power-game when you need something from him. That tiny bit of power to keep you waiting, or make you beg for help, can be seen every-where. In some southwestern towns, people drive at half the speed limit so they have the power to make everyone behind them angry, and they drive up and down the main street to make sure they can affect as many others as possible.

This childish craving for power may seem laughable to most of us, but it may also serve a purpose for those afflicted with it. There is nothing more dangerous than a man with no self-esteem. He cannot be happy. Everyone else seems to be in control of their lives, even if it isn't so.

The police enforce the laws, the boss makes rules for the job, the wife makes the rules at home, and the poor fellow may be the slave of a bottle, cigarettes and caffeine. This guy may explode and take a few others down with him. Without small everyday releases, the volcano will erupt someday.

Hitler was a failure at most things he tried. He wanted to be an architect, but was harshly judged as a failure. His story of pain and hatred shows a frightening truth about LOSERS. They get very jealous of WINNERS, in his case the intelligent and successful Jews, and seek revenge in desperate ways. Losers are not necessarily satisfied with equality, they want to be recognized as superior.

Politics and religions have given some of the greatest cripples the means to get revenge. So many wars have been fought for the GLORY of some king or queen, for the father or mother land, to convert the non-believers to spread some stupid belief or another. It is time to step out of this madness.

There is no possibility of gaining TOTAL power over the world around you. The competition is tough because so many others want recognition. The small amount of power you can accumulate is only temporal. Life will go on long after you are dead and forgotten.

I once met a New Ager who believed in POSITIVE THINKING. He had programmed himself to think about whatever it was he wanted, and to try not to think of anything bad. This guy was a mess. He was so scared that he might cause something horrible to happen by thinking it. If he'd wish to get some money, he feared that his grandmother might die to leave it to him.

One night, after watching him pace around the room for an hour looking out the window because he was worried that someone might break into his car, I asked him to sit down and try something with me. He was skeptical, knowing that I am a mischief, but he finally agreed.

I told him to imagine that three tough guys were out at his car right now. He grew uptight. "Now, see them pull out chains and start smashing in all your windows!"

"What?" he cried. "It will happen!"

"Now imagine they are pouring gasoline over the seats and one of them throws in a match. BOOM!"

He recoiled as if it was really happening. "Okay," I finished, "Now go see that it hasn't happened and you can relax."

The paradox of power over others is that it can only happen when the dominated GIVES his power away to the dominator. Any dictator or president can only rule those who recognize them as leaders. A religious leader is nothing unless he gathers a bunch of sheep, but the sheep have to be willing. They want spiritual security, leaving the responsibility to the priest, but it is a foolish choice.

No one can give you spirituality. No book can TELL the truth, not even this one. All that can be done is to HINT at the experience and offer possible methods. There can be no guarantee that you will have a similar experience because each of us has developed our own blocks to clear vision.

What about metaphysical powers? Mystics have recognized for centuries that mystical powers are another TRAP. Certainly there are powers available to those who wish to develop them, but it is again a desire to be special. Whether the seeker wants to be a healer, or tell the future, levitate or materialize objects, it's all another ego-trip.

In the mid-seventies, I became involved with the American Indian path, finding myself remembering words, customs and rituals of the Blackfeet Indians, as if I'd lived that life before.

I've never written about this period of my life before. Even though I am revealing my experiences to you, I ask that you don't BELIEVE what I am telling you, but merely hear it. Anybody can write anything and can fool you. This is the truth as I experienced it and maybe some of my insights will prove valuable to you.

During that five-year period, 1974-1979, I became a rainmaker and healer. Wherever I went, the rain would follow and I could call on it to come. My friends learned not to invite me to outdoor gatherings unless they had shelter. Powers are available which cannot be understood, but there is always a catch, an equal and opposite reaction to every action, as I'll explain.

I attended the First Annual Rocky Mountain Healing Festival in 1976 where I learned reflexology, iridology, psychic healing techniques and much more. It was the beginning of the NEW AGE movement which crept into mainstream America nearly ten years later. (By that time I was out of it.)

I had already been playing with psychokinesis, moving objects with energy and healing plants, but I began working with people. By entering into an altered state of consciousness, I found I could literally MELT tumors, heal sprains and remove headaches. It took a great deal of my energy to achieve these healings, but I felt I was doing the right thing, helping others.

After speaking to a class at the local college, I was approached by a man who said his uncle had been in a coma for over eight months and asked if I would try to help him. All the medical professionals had given up on this guy and he was in a rest home. I agreed to try. Without getting into the details, which would take a whole book, the man popped out of the coma four days after my visit and I was instantly a celebrity, receiving letters from everywhere asking me to come do MIRACLES for their ailments. This made me a bit shaky as I knew I couldn't do all of them, I never accepted any money for the service and I could see this was becoming a great ego-trip.

The first clue that I was INTERFERING with something unknown was when a girl I had healed of uterine cancer came back six months later, bragging about two new deadly diseases she'd contracted. Something deep inside me realized that I was not really healing anyone, but using my willpower to change the form of the problem. Maybe these sicknesses were necessary for that person to grow, or maybe she intentionally grew ill to get attention. Either way, I knew I wasn't ready to go pro.

I later learned that the man who had been in the coma never lifted a hand to help himself and became a burden to his family, complaining and demanding constant care. One boy said, "He should have died." Again, I could see that my playing with power was not only draining me, but disrupting some unseen balance. I was taking away my patients' responsibilities for their own health and happiness and placing myself above them.

I know from these experiences that we all can influence some of the events that surround us and various ailments in our bodies. Many forms of modern healing depend on regaining the will to be healthy, but they keep you involved in trying to change reality.

A deeper insight is needed to TRANSFORM yourself to be accepting of whatever existence offers. Then all your actions become part of the universal energies. It may sound like a loss of freedom, but it is really the beginning of the only REAL freedom, freedom to be part of the WHOLE, beyond the confines of the ego. All just IS and we are part of it.

When I saw that I was getting caught in powers, I dropped everything and began a sincere search for reality. Without exception, I can say that any sincere search, with awareness and love, will lead you back to yourself.

I still heal plants and sometimes headaches or other minor disturbances, but I learned to ACCEPT even a broken back when it happened to me. The meditator looks for the GIFT in everything instead of trying to change it to fit their expectations. What to do with a broken back? I began writing.

In Ramakrishna's time, there was a man who had studied many years to learn how to walk on water. He came to Ramakrishna, who was well-known, to show off his superior power. The man asked Ramakrishna to come walk with him on the water and discuss spiritual matters.

But Ramakrishna was enlightened and knew the dangers of power. He invited the man to come walk on the clouds and talk. Of course the man couldn't walk on the clouds and grew angry.

Ramakrishna asked the man how long it had taken him to learn how to walk on water. The answer was thirty years.

"Amazing," said Ramakrishna. "I can go to the ferry man and ride across the river for half a rupee. Your powers are only worth half a rupee!"

Mystical powers pull you back into the outside world, into the involvement with respectability and the opinions of others. They cannot help you to find the deepest truths in yourself. Anyone who uses trickery to gather disciples, is committing a CRIME. When it is revealed that the magic was just tricks, the seeker will feel ripped off and might stop seeking. False masters are in the majority. Be alert!

There is another power which is often overlooked: the power of love. Have you ever seen the transformative power of love? It can turn a wounded heart into a brilliant star, cure many diseases without effort, and it enriches both the giver and the given. Just remember that it is very fragile and needs to be handled gently.

Love flows through every pore of your body, every moment of your life. Meditation brings awareness of that strength and can spark it in greater amounts as your heart matures. Love reconnects you to your center, your very source of life. The power of the heart is for inner mastery. The surrounding world may be affected by you, but it is not due to any EFFORT on your part. Your love and joy simply INVITE others to enter their own temples, within themselves.

A CREATIVE REBEL recognizes only the power to be himself. With that freedom comes the recognition that all others also need to be themselves. There is no rush to gain recognition and to prove anyone else to be inferior. Competition breeds hatred. Comparison creates jealousy.

This spiritual power comes through the experience of the heart and awareness of the being. It must be felt, lived and tasted by each person individually. It cannot be handed to another and no one can accompany you on the journey to your center. One who has reached the center can create devices to help snap the grip of the mind on you, but the truth is already within, waiting only for you to DISCOVER it.

You can even evolve out of the powers your body has over you. The unconscious sex drive, the anger and fear, all the emotions that rule your life can be transformed. I am not condemning these emotions; they are the seeds. But don't stay with the seeds, bring in consciousness to every aspect of your life and the tree will grow.

Love has a power over the heart of which many people are afraid. In an effort to remain safe, they may even be attracted to people who are incapable of returning their love. Being entangled with a husband or wife who is abusive introduces the role of the VICTIM, who takes no responsibility for the situation, and may successfully bring sympathy from friends.

With consciousness, love becomes another entrance to your own center. Maybe the word ADORE can mean "a door". The more mature love becomes, the less it is affected by others. The power of love melts us back into union with existence.

Many different forms of the will-to-power are discussed in the various chapters of this book, but they all boil down to one cause: feelings of inferiority and weakness. To grow out of the need for attention and acceptance, you will need to find your innermost power SOURCE, from which your life energies spring.

A medieval king was out hunting with his best knight and a servant when the party became lost. The servant was sent to find the way out of the forest. Coming upon an old blind man sitting with a child, the servant yelled, "In the name of the king, tell me which way leads out of the woods or I'll cut off your heads!"

The old man pointed the way and the servant disappeared.

Soon, the knight was sent to find the way out and came upon the same old man and child. "Pardon me, sir, please show me the way out of this forest," the knight said.

Again, the old man showed him the way and the knight went ahead. The king eventually wandered into the same clearing. "I am lost," the king said. "Might you help this old fool find his way out of the forest?"

"Yes, Your Majesty," the old man replied. "Your servant and knight have just gone ahead of you."

When the king had gone, the boy asked the blind man, "But how did you know which was which?"

"Only the weak, the servant would have threatened us. Only a brave knight would have been so polite in asking a lowly peasant. And only the king himself could have accepted total responsibility for getting himself lost."

CHAPTER FIFTEEN

SATANISM-
THE DEVIL WITH YOU

An abundance of recent television "news" shows have been dedicated to Satanism as a growing problem, especially with teenagers. They claim that Heavy Metal music is responsible for advocating Devil worship to a young and impressionable audience, but there is much more to it than that.

Roxanna Alday, music editor of *WESTWORD* magazine in Denver, told me in a recent interview that many of the Heavy Metal musicians use Satan as a symbol of defiance, but have no intention of influencing their audience into fanaticism. "The reason the politicians are labelling this music SATANIC is that they fear it," Roxanna told me. "It expresses truth, criticizes hypocrisy and institutions, and it is justly angry and powerful."

One of the top Satanic musicians is called King Diamond. He explains that one of his concerts, filled with morbid imagery, is like seeing a horror movie. "I don't believe that you can influence kids that easily, because if you could, then you would have everybody shooting each other after watching the news."

Heavy Metal is CATHARTIC music and can help to throw off frustrations if you have few other opportunities to explode. An offshoot of Heavy Metal is called THRASH music. It is very political and angry, pointing fingers at the society for letting money corrupt our freedoms, for destroying the ecology, and painting fearful images of another war to end the Earth. It's a great way to transform aggressions into creative movement. Just add meditative AWARENESS at the end and you'll have my vote.

Many young people are angry, finding themselves born into a world of hypocrites who seem bent on destroying our planet. To express and vent this frustration, the music forms are changing. From my experience, release is necessary to be sane and I don't see that many young Heavy Metal fans are interested in blood sacrifice or the "Christian Devil". They enjoy being frightened by the spectacle of this wild entertainment.

A few individuals with previous mental problems, and often drug problems, have drawn the focus of the media because they have committed murder in disturbing Satanic rituals. These incidents are exceptional and are usually preceded by signs of mental illness.

Satanism was originally a creation of the priests, as is every organized religion. By choosing to divide life into good and bad, sin and saintliness, the priests have laid the groundwork for Satanism. It is the logical conclusion of the good/bad dichotomy. Devil and divine come from the same root.

In the beginning, there was the priest. By creating the concept of God as a DISCIPLINARIAN, watching your every move to see if you should be allowed to enter his heaven, the priest could instill fear of being judged unworthy and left out. The Devil takes it one step further; here is the ruler of the underworld who will be there to punish you for eternity if you haven't followed the rules.

What kind of mind could fabricate such a horrible place as the Christian hell? And for ETERNITY, not just a few years' sentence. Look in the Bible and see the descriptions of hell. It is filled with perverted sex, torture, and fire. Have all the priests gone there to see it, or has this hell developed in their minds from centuries of repressing themselves?

Satanism is a reaction to the oppression of organized religion. It is the ultimate "NO" to parents and teachers. The Devil was used as a device to scare people into obeying, and now a few reactionaries have chosen to revolt against the system and "serve the Devil".

This Devil fellow promises power to his worshippers. Once again, who needs power? Only someone who feels powerless; someone who feels inferior to others. Teenagers often feel utterly powerless. Who listens to you?

But Satanism cannot give power any more than Santa Claus can give you a pet pony. Satan is a fiction. He is the personification of fear, and fear is a closing of the heart. Fear is a DEVICE used to control potential rebels. Satan was originally conceived to scare both children and adults to keep them interested in the protection offered by the church. Love is the missing factor. An open heart radiates trust, not fear.

Almost every culture has developed ingenious ways to control their children so they aren't such a disturbance and prone to disobedience. Some Pueblo Indians used Kachinas, men dressed as Gods who would dance through the village. The mothers would point to the beast and tell their children, "If you don't behave, that Kachina will come to get you!"

Once the kids have seen this monster, they are sure that he exists. Later, during the puberty rites, the young boys are tested by facing the Kachina, who might whip them with a willow sprig. If a boy proves to be brave and passes the test, the whipper would take off his costume and reveal his identity. The initiate would then be allowed to whip the man who has fooled him.

Some African tribes used a bull-roarer, a device swung around the head which makes a ferocious noise. Neither the women nor the children were allowed to see the source of the noise and would be frightened until the men "chased the beast away." The men proved their protectiveness and were considered to be heroes.

Using FEAR to control people cannot lead to true religiousness. Being afraid of falling into hell, or greedy for an afterlife in heaven, is only manipulation of base instincts. When the manipulated discover their lives are being dominated, they react.

Satanism, as a religion, is REACTIVE. Back when the church ruled the lives of almost everyone, Satanism was a revolution against the oppressive religious orders. It worked. Satanism caused so much fear that the priests murdered millions of people, mostly women, if there was even a suspicion of stepping out of line with the church. The 200 years of Crusades and the Inquisition of the

Thirteenth Century together sparked more bloodshed and torture than any known war before it.

In Satanism, the churches' hold on people's minds has backfired. Instead of being GOOD and confessing to sins, which are condemned natural behavior, some people have chosen to become totally BAD, participating in human sacrifices to a fictitious Devil. What a mess!

Today, Satanism seems to appeal more to those who have other problems as well, such as hard drug addiction. Drugs magnify dreams. While under the influence of drugs, one might encounter the projection of the Devil himself and be more apt to commit crimes, even murders, than a clear-thinking person would.

Churches have labelled sex, and anything else which is natural, as sin. Since sex is in all of us, the churches try to keep us feeling guilty and wanting forgiveness. But we all know sex is there, in all of us, and a mixed-up person may then conclude that Satan is tempting him. All the prayer in the world won't change the fact that we are sexual beings. It is nature's way, and nature is considered to be God's work.

Each Satanic group, I understand, has to have a priest at the core, a priest who has converted from God to Satan. It is really the same belief system, up-side down. The only way back to sanity is to throw the whole system.

Beliefs are only skin deep. No one KNOWS if what they believe in is right or not. Choosing to believe in Christ or Krishna or Allah cannot transform your doubts. It can only cover them. A person who has been taught to believe blindly, can easily believe in anything, even the Devil.

To accept that nature is NOT evil is the first step toward conquering this mental disease. Nature is exactly as existence has made you. If you want to call the creative force God, then God has created us as part of nature. Sex is the act of creating new life, which should be considered a sacred act, a chance to feel and share love.

Those who are FINANCIALLY dependent on mass beliefs will oppose anyone who discovers the truth. Those who wish everyone to be dependent on them and who wish to dictate what reality should be, will strike out against those who cause their followers to doubt their teachings and scriptures. Maybe nothing else condemns more than calling another "Satanic".

Satanism is part of the two-year-old "NO" stage. There are so many ways to release this pent-up anger and negativity without hurting anyone, as I've explained earlier. Hatred can never lead to anything but destruction.

Satanism is absolutely negative. A natural person, who allows his life to unfold without repression, could not be attracted to it. Who cares about power when you are in love? Why would anyone want to hurt another when his whole life is a benediction?

I foresee an end to Satanism concurring with an end to ALL organized belief systems. Our planet cannot survive much longer with the antiquated ideologies of organized religions. We have to become intelligent enough to look beyond teachings and prejudice and see life as it really is. Our future lies in INDIVIDUAL religious experience.

All the religions of the past have claimed to have the TRUTH as if it is a commodity. To keep individuals from going within and finding real truth, these religions have pointed outwardly, emphasizing actions such as service, prayer, and afterlife. Looking outwardly can only take you away from yourself. Knowing ABOUT truth can't help you discover your own being; you have to BE the truth.

A young devil comes running to the Hot One with bad news. "Hey, Satan, someone has just found himself and is spreading love around the world. What can we do?"

"Don't worry," says Beelzebub. "My people have already reached there."

"But", says the little devil, "I just came from there and he was surrounded only by priests."

"I know," Satan laughs. "Those are MY people."

CHAPTER SIXTEEN

STREET WISE?

The streets of our largest cities were designed as pathways to get from one place to another, and were never meant to be places to LIVE. That such a multitude of refugees live there is one of the saddest truths of our times, especially in a country which is so proud of its wealth and freedom.

For the many teenagers who have run away from home, the streets have become a nightmare of day-to-day survival. They fall prey to exploiters on every corner. Drug pushers, pimps, prostitutes, and thieves offer ways to survive, and to DIE.

Running away from a bad scene at home can mean getting lost in a jungle of perverted sex, drugs and violence. There may not have been much love at home, but there is less on city streets. What are the alternatives?

Sometimes the choice of running away produces a no-return situation. The house you left might be closed to you, or the abusive punishment for running may be too unbearable to go back. So, the first option is not to run away in the first place. There are usually better choices than sleeping on the street.

Try to get help from outside the immediate family. Maybe there is a friend or relative who will understand your problems and offer at least a temporary refuge. Most towns and cities have special phone numbers listed for battered wives and children. If you feel you are really being threatened by staying at home, it's better to call and check it out than to condemn yourself to roam the Siberian streets.

If you are reading this and are already on the street, you must know about the shelters for runaways. Covenant House and other church run homes are possibilities. Thousands of runaways have sought and received help there. Just because they are run by a church doesn't mean you have to be assailed with religious jabber and pressure to conform.

Many of the street people I've interviewed have complained about the forced religious activities of the Salvation Army, if you need to stay there. Before being offered a meal and a cot for the night, some have been forced to listen to an hour of insulting religious jabber, with the hosts condemning their guests as sinners and screaming for conversion.

Anyone with a religious motive is not really there to HELP you, but only to convert you. This is not real service. Orphans are gathered off the street Mother Theresa-style, so they can become converts of the religious order which has grabbed them. It may well be better than starving, but it is psychological exploitation, not the pure compassionate service they claim to be giving.

I can't write about all the indignities suffered on the streets because there are too many, but I can suggest that young adults who are in trouble can be creative enough to locate a nurturing environment for refuge instead of getting stuck without even a high school diploma on a street with few legal jobs worth doing.

It is also necessary to note that the cities are the most EXPENSIVE places to live. That which may sustain you well elsewhere becomes a bare minimum, even if you work and try to rent an apartment. The same money could give you a comfortable living in a rural area, if you could find a job there.

Many teenagers who left home in the sixties found that they could band together and rent a house which none of them could afford alone. If enough participants are found who will really appreciate the communal living conditions and take good care of the house, this can be a viable alternative to street life.

Within most cities, there are means of public transportation which enable us to get around without cars. To purchase a car, keep it in good running shape, get insurance, buy gasoline, oil and all, takes a steady job. Driving can also be dangerous, especially for the less-experienced. If a car is needed, then a group purchase can again be an alternative. As long as each driver is on the insurance policy and agrees not to drive after using alcohol or drugs, this can work. Unfortunately, many teens think they can handle a few drinks and still drive and there are many cemetery headstones in every city which prove they were wrong.

Running away before you have a high school education and possibility of making a living can only be an option to the most desperate teens. There are many programs to help bring parents and teens together, to get back to communication and hopefully create an understanding. All have to give a little if they wish to meet. Maybe try one of these programs before committing yourself to the hard life of the street.

Parents may be pushing their children too hard, with all good INTENTIONS. Their intentions may only be that their children should get a good education so they will succeed. After so many years of being a parent, they have run out of patience, while the teenagers have learned more sophisticated ways to push parental buttons.

After having been a child, and treated like one for your whole life, you want to be given more freedoms to choose. Hey, it's a difficult age. The adult within has not yet any experience, and the child has not quite let go. Teens are not given the trust and rights of grown-ups, but they are no longer helpless little children either.

I am perfectly aware that there are horrible situations possible at HOME. Parents who beat or sexually abuse their sons and daughters make life a nightmare for the victims of their insanities. Getting out of the house may be your only chance for survival.

If you are being ABUSED by a parent or other person in the household, don't give up and feel helpless, seek help. Every school has advisors who are there to help you. In most cities and towns, you can call Social Services, possibly called Human Services in the phone book. There may also be a separate number for The Child Protective Agency. These people are experts at helping.

In most cases, it is better to call these social workers than to call the police, unless there is immediate danger. Let the social workers call in specific policepersons who are sympathetic and trained in these matters, if needed.

It's ridiculous to feel guilty or ashamed because you have been mistreated. You need not protect the person who has hurt you either, there are laws to protect you from further abuse and from unjust punishment.

If you are really stuck in a bad situation, call for help. But remember, the responsibility is always yours. If you have chosen to run away, or you are now choosing to stay away, it is YOUR decision.

Consider the alternatives. Do you want to live with Foster parents? It might be better than home. Would you be more comfortable in a group home? Can you wait a few years until you can support yourself and move away from home without an intense struggle?

The TRUE REBEL is at home wherever he goes. Being resourceful, listening to the silence within, the rebel carries his treasure of joy wherever he goes. The laughter that meditation brings can transform a group home or any other house into a fun place.

There is NO possibility of a true rebel selling his body sexually on the street. Especially now with AIDS, he would rather go to a shelter than die on the streets in such slavery.

Drug running is a similar fate. You may not get addicted to the wares, but you may get addicted to the lifestyle. Eventually, the addicts you sell to will get desperate, maybe enough to kill you for more dope. Dealers get into trouble with police and with rival gangs. Theft is always a motive for murder.

So, if you have been thinking life is ROUGH on the home-front, just imagine how much harder it is "out there". Check out all the alternatives before you start a life where crime is needed to survive. Attend a teen-support seminar, talk to the school guidance counselor, or get help from other adults in a position to help you.

If you're out on the street and in trouble, you can call the Teen Runaway Hotline anywhere in the USA 1-800-621-4000. No one needs to be abused, especially while she is still young. Seek help from those who are offering it. Be intelligent. The only way to be street-wise is not to live there!

CHAPTER SEVENTEEN

GETTING IN TROUBLE

It's kind of a tradition that teenagers should get into hot water once in a while as you try new things and discover which ones you don't want to repeat. But, why do you suppose some individuals manage to get into trouble no matter what they do?

Little children learn one trick, that doing what you've been told NOT to do gets you lots of attention. It may be negative attention, but it is attention none-the-less.

Positive attention is not so easy to get. If you do as you've been told, you are accepted, but parents seldom call for an award ceremony to honor your obedience, if they notice at all. Going along with everything you are told feels a bit like selling-out. You have no control over decisions made for you.

Negative attention gets the JUICES flowing. Everybody loses their composure; you have let them down. There is an underlying feeling of having the power to object, to say NO. The parent or boss may yell and scream, knowing they have lost control of you.

It is a natural part of growing into an individual to go against parents and teachers. Growth takes guts and a lot of energy and teens have both. If you always follow the rules and do as you're told, you can never feel free and responsible. Most parents, and societies, claim that punishment is "for your own good". This is often just a RATIONALIZATION to cover up the fact that you have disobeyed and they want revenge. Who has ever learned anything by punishment? Only more hatred and pain come out of it.

Jesus used to tell a parable about a shepherd who had one hundred sheep until the largest ran away. The shepherd left the ninety-nine to search for the largest and when he found him, he told the sheep, "I love thee more than the ninety-nine".

Jesus was a rebel. He is saying that the best, the largest, will ALWAYS leave the flock, the masses. In fact, only the best will have the guts to go astray. Only the most intelligent child will make trouble when he is told to do something. In his own metaphorical way, Jesus is saying that you have to go astray to really come home. He was crucified for his rebelliousness.

A Zen master used to commit crimes right in front of the police station and would be thrown into prison. As soon as he was released, he would do it again. When asked about his strange behavior, the Master replied that he could only find the caliber of people who could become enlightened in the prison. These people had gone astray and could now come home.

Once in a while it may be healthy and fun to be BAD; ask Michael Jackson. A Walt Disney movie I saw as a child stated, "Nothing tastes better than a stolen watermelon." Of course, later the boys find out they've stolen the farmer's prize watermelon and see the pain they've caused.

Tom Sawyer and Huckleberry Finn have been two of the best-loved characters in America. They are both rebels, fighting authority figures, and doing quite as they please. There is an acceptance in Mark Twain's writings that "boys will be boys".

So, what will girls be? Pippi Longstocking is a child who lives without parents in a large house. She owns a horse and a monkey. Pippi has the power to lift almost anything, and enough money to have many friends. She gives sweets to other kids so they'll do what she wants instead of what the teacher wants.

Pippi wears outrageous clothing, keeps her house a mess since no one can make her clean it up, and sleeps with her shoes on. She wins arguments by creating her own confusing logic, which no man can understand. She is free, clever and displays the power most kids want to have themselves.

I don't know if these books are still popular with today's youth, but the same wishes for power and freedom are obviously contemporary. Even the Bible exhibits the understanding that whatever is FORBIDDEN becomes attractive, as in the case of Adam and Eve. If God hadn't pointed it out to them, they might have never discovered the "forbidden fruits".

Our society has its own forbidden fruits which it protects with laws. All laws are stated to be for the good of the people, or the state, but then why are there different laws in every country? Are there universal concepts of right and wrong, or not?

Laws dealing with assault and murder are invented to protect people from aggression. PUNISHMENT has been the accepted method for dealing with lawbreakers, but hopefully it will be changing soon. As science has unwound the mysteries of the mind, they have found chemical imbalances may be the causes of most violent crimes. The new question is whether to treat murderers as criminals or as mentally ill.

Years ago, retarded people were locked up and punished for being different. All kinds of devices were invented by religious idiots to "chase the devil out". With our new understanding of mental illness, many retarded people are allowed to live happy and productive lives.

Our prisons are really universities where small-time offenders are sent to study with the experts. Being locked up with con-men and thieves, possibly being sexually abused and beaten, is not going to solve the problem of being anti-social.

Punishment also leaves the offender with a bitter taste in his mouth and an urge for VENGEANCE. He may have become an outlaw to support his family. Can a prison term cure poverty? The family may be forced to continue in crime to survive without him. When he is released, the society shuns him and he may be forced into crime again.

Once you've been in trouble with the law, it limits your ability to ever work again. Businesses want to know your criminal record before agreeing to hire you. Most of the jobs available to uneducated or untrained people don't pay enough to live well, and there is again the temptation to steal.

I love the story of Lao Tzu, the ancient Chinese Sage. He was once summoned to the court of the Emperor and told his wisdom was to be used as a court judge. Lao Tzu agreed to try, but warned the Emperor that it would only last a few days at the most.

The first case was brought before Lao Tzu. A rich man had been robbed and was bringing the thief in for sentencing. Lao Tzu sentenced the thief to six months in jail and the RICH MAN to six years in jail! The Emperor was called in. The rich man was one of his greatest supporters and even the Emperor owed him money.

"What have you done?" asked the Emperor.

"It is simple," Lao Tzu declared. "The thief has done wrong and must serve six months for his crime. The rich man has done a much greater wrong. He has become rich by making thousands of others poor. The poor man had to steal to live. The rich man is the real criminal."

Of course, Lao Tzu was allowed to leave the palace and never was called to be a judge again as his insights went far beyond the laws of his society. Most courts give the offender nothing but revenge for not conforming to the society, and revenge can only spark more hatred.

It's also possible that a man may turn to crime because he can't accept the compromises needed to live in his society. Some of the most intelligent people may be in our ever-growing prisons because they were never offered a way to survive as individuals.

Love and understanding may have been missing in the lives of those who turn to crime. Positive alternatives are needed instead of punishment. Punishment should be a crime. Criminals need HELP and UNDERSTANDING, not retribution.

Just as intelligent children fight with their parents for individuality, a criminal may be reacting the same way with the larger parents, the society. Failure to fit in is not necessarily a problem. Many of us misfits have found ways to channel our energies into CREATIVITY.

My own understanding is that LAWS are made because LOVE is missing. A person in love won't harm others. Rules have to be given to those who've never found inner love and kindness. A man who has been mistreated all his life will naturally mistreat others. The cycle goes on becoming worse when hurt and unloved people turn to crime and are treated with hatred and punishment.

It may be possible in the near future to treat criminals with tenderness and understanding, with psychology, and with injections of chemicals to balance mental problems. Compassion may work better than JUSTICE and revenge.

Destruction is easy. Any child can do it. It takes no special talent to destroy things, but it takes much talent to create. Painting graffiti on buildings or vandalizing other people's property is pure destruction. If all that energy spent on destruction in one day was put into creativity ...

Like it or not, people have the right to OWN property and there are laws to protect it. Only a few things are common property in this culture, such as public utilities and parks. Even these have to be protected from angry kids who want to get even with the society which gave them a raw deal. Why should others enjoy the park when you haven't even enough bread to eat?

Perhaps a teenager is fed up with the suppression of his parents and decides to do something bad, just for fun. Halloween pranks are a good source of "blowing off steam" as long as they don't destroy anything. The rebel of which I speak cannot intentionally hurt others in the name of fun. He will not let anger build up to that degree.

Anger leads to destruction, or it can supply the basic energy to better your situation. Humans are extremely creative unless they have been taught to think of themselves as failures. Creative activities are supported in many ways by the society itself. Find a project that works and, together with others who want to succeed, you'll make it.

Of course, you can find yourself in big trouble without looking for it. As girls mature physically, they may attract the attentions of repressed boys. Add a little alcohol and you have the makings of a date-rape.

There are precautions you can take to prevent being attacked such as dating in small GROUPS, staying in public places, and carrying a whistle or mace. Still, a situation can happen unexpectedly and you may find yourself being overpowered by an out-of-control sexually obsessed football player.

There is no right or wrong thing to do. Use your head. Try to talk your way out. If that fails, try to get away. Offer a condom if all else fails, at least you won't get pregnant. To fight with an attacker and lose, you may not only be raped, but beaten also. If you are raped, GET HELP. Tell others and try to get help for the sex offender before he strikes again.

Many children are sexually abused in the home, by parents and other members of the family. They may be afraid to tell others, because it seems shameful and they are scared. Any kind of abuse will leave scars on you and healing will take love and understanding, which you won't get without telling someone who cares. Talk with others who've had similar experiences.

Boys can also find themselves attacked, often by other boys. Bullies usually run in packs and outnumber their victims. Any excuse can lead to a beating; even race, religion, which school or gang you are thought to belong to, or just because you walked down the wrong street. Strangely enough, Blacks usually murder Blacks, Hispanics kill other Hispanics, etc. Murder is one of the leading causes of death among teenagers today.

Defending yourself can be a problem. Not all of us are black belt karate experts or Mutant Ninja Turtles. The main thing is to keep your center and be intelligent. Wait for a break.

I was once jumped while hitchhiking (the LAST time I ever tried hitching!) by three Hispanics who mistook me for a white (instead of a human being). They were quite drunk and took me into the woods for a little Friday night fun. I fought with them for a while, but soon realized that I was losing pretty badly. All three were sitting on me, beating me with bottles in the face and head.

I kept asking them why they were doing this. Couldn't they see I was a brother? I guess they couldn't. I finally stopped struggling and relaxed, doing deep breathing to regain some energy. The next bottle smashed over my head and I was knocked out. Or was I? I pretended to be unconscious and they let go of my arms. That was all I needed to bolt to my feet and escape into the darkness.

My point is that you can usually find a way out if you stay centered. I learned a lot from that situation. Instead of trusting everybody, I learned to trust my intuition, to trust life; but NOT to be stupid. Avoid situations where you are outnumbered without an escape. There is nothing to prove by fighting.

Learn to shut up when a large angry person is choosing to beat you instead of a pillow. Many girls get beaten because they keep pushing a huge man until he snaps. Is it better to try winning an argument at that cost, or be quiet and prevent being abused?

Trouble is part of the world and there is no escape from being in some kind of trouble. Just remember that you'll have your whole life to continue playing if you don't look for trouble and get yourself extinguished.

A rebel has to be intelligent. Going against rules is not always a sign of individuality. Some rules are NEEDED to coexist with large groups of people, such as traffic rules. If you decide to make your own traffic rules, you'll only prove how stupid you are. Organizational rules like these protect everyone and they evolved out of need.

Every culture differs from other cultures because of location, background, religious conditioning, and accepted social behavior. Even traffic laws vary. The traffic laws of England are opposite from those in the USA because driving on the left symbolizes loyalty to the Queen and Americans chose to rebel.

I've always found it fun to blow people's minds by stepping out of expected behavior, sort of making creative trouble. One time, when I was driving along in my 1954 Chevy pickup in Santa Fe, I came upon a cop with a flat tire on his cruiser. I pulled off the road and asked if he needed help. The cop said he didn't have a jack and had radioed for aid.

Noting the suspicion he felt for me, with my long hair and beard, I decided to surprise him. Pulling the jack from my truck, I proceeded to change his tire while the dumbfounded cop looked on. Just as I finished my work and danced off to my truck, singing, another cop finally arrived and I could hear them talking.

"Who the hell was that?" asked new arrival.

"I don't know," said the first cop. "Some hippie just drove up and changed my tire."

This kind of trouble can heal the world.

One teenager has written me, asking for advice after she let her drunk boyfriend drive an uninsured car that was lent to her. He drove it off a washed-out bridge. Just accepting an uninsured car was irresponsible. Letting the boyfriend drive seems to be unconsciously asking for serious trouble. She was so lucky no one was killed.

For a rebel, there is no question of responsibility. The uninsured car would have been refused. The drunk boyfriend was only given the wheel because she wanted him to like her, but a REBEL is not concerned with popularity. Take full responsibility for your life and you are free, no question of who's in charge, YOU are!

Now this same girl has turned her life around. She got her GED and wants to go to college to study psychology. She is doing whatever she wants to do with her life. Being a CREATIVE REBEL doesn't mean you never make mistakes, it means you never make the same mistakes twice.

PS- Youth Crisis Hotline Tel. 1 800 621-4000 toll free.

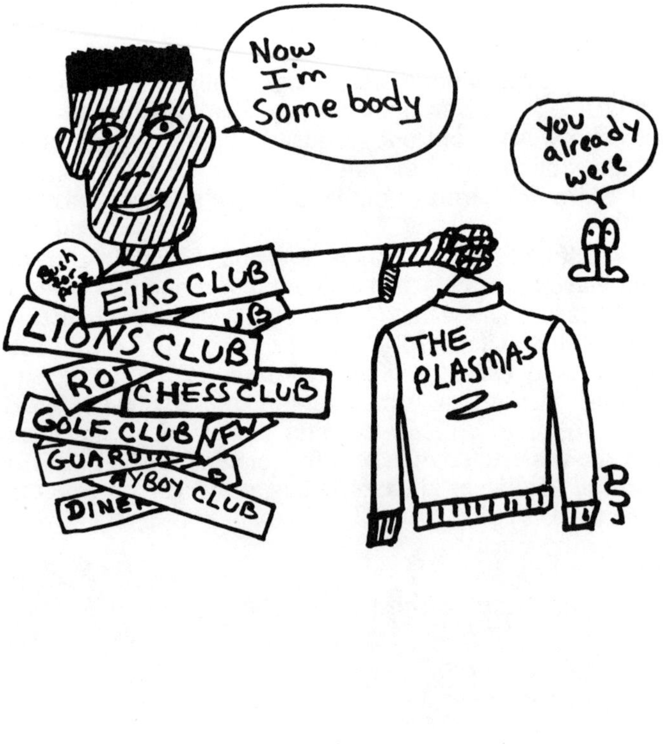
Now I'm Somebody
you already were
EIKS CLUB
LIONS CLUB
CHESS CLUB
GOLF CLUB
VFW
THE PLASMAS

CHAPTER EIGHTEEN

OUR GANG

For those who live in cities, whether on the streets or not, there is always the presence of GANGS. Some gangs are just groups of friends who hang out together and have fun, protecting each other from aggression. Other gangs are based in hatred and are out to fight, rape, and even kill.

One of the most unfortunate aspect of a gang is the peer pressure. Those who are unsure of their MANLINESS or courage might join a gang to feel safe. With an entire group of cowards joined together, there may be pressure to prove how daring they are by committing vicious acts, much the same way college fraternities may TEST new members with insane tortures.

Teenage gangs often provide opportunities to show how stupid you can be to get approval. Doing hard drugs, stealing cars, hurting those who are weaker than you; many are the ways to become a slave. Do you really want the acceptance of vicious idiots?

Cowardly WEAKLINGS are the most dangerous people on the Earth. Anyone with inner strength will not have to prove how tough he is. In a gang, many weak individuals are able to cover their fears by bullying others, with the power of their numbers. The most cowardly are responsible for the drive-by shootings we hear about all the time or the skin heads attacking minorities.

Forming a gang is a very PRIMITIVE concept. Humans are not alone in forming small groups of individuals who travel together for protection. Usually the weaker the animal, the larger the gang. Deer and sheep have to stay together because they have little means of defense other than fast getaways.

Coyotes and wolves can be alone, but cooperate in hunting for the benefit of the group. Large hunting cats like to go it alone. They don't need the pack to slow them down.

In the same way, MYSTICS have compared different aspects of human beings to animals. The SHEEP-people always do whatever the group does. They try to be secure by fitting in and following. The crowd and the masses are just other names for sheep-people.

The LIONS are the loners. Not needing to be surrounded by a group, the lion thinks for himself. An enlightened master is so in tune with the universe that he emits an energy field, even though he might not even defend himself if attacked.

I've always loved the story about the lion who was born among sheep. He learned to eat grass, "baaah" like a sheep, and to run whenever danger was near. One day, a huge male lion came to drink and saw the small lion grazing with the sheep. He couldn't believe his eyes! A lion was running away screaming like a sheep.

After much chasing, the old lion finally caught the youth and dragged him down to the lake. There he showed the youth his real face in the reflection. The young lion looked in amazement, then gave a mighty roar!

This is the the birth of the rebel. Just seeing that your potential is that of an EMPEROR, how can you remain a BEGGAR? A rebel will not fit in with the sheep again no matter how he tries. Gangs are not for rebels.

Whenever a mob exists, crying for some great change or other, there is going to be a group MIND, the collective unconsciousness. A mob acts in ways that the individuals within the mob could not act alone. With all the excitement and others egging them on, individuals can find themselves doing things that they know are wrong. As part of a crowd, the individual loses personal responsibility and the crowd becomes answerable for the actions.

A rebel cannot be part of any mob, even if he agrees with their cause. Wherever he goes, the rebel is utterly himself, even in the middle of a crowded market place. All of us are really alone, and the rebel accepts the reality of it. He remains his own master. He decides what is right or wrong for himself. There is no way to tell what is right for someone else. A rebel will not try to force another to go against his feelings either. The focus for a rebel is INWARD. Only he can create what goes into his mind once he becomes aware enough to dissolve the trash placed there by others.

A recent study by anthropologist Marvin Harris points out that for 98% of our evolution, mankind has formed small nomadic bands of 30-50 individuals. Harris has found that the surviving groups he studied all show a lack of hierarchy. Africans, South Americans, and North American Indians may have respected the advice of an elder or great hunter, but there was no power to ORDER anyone.

A society without chiefs, says Harris, was the basic society of the past. Among the !Kung bushmen of the Kalahari, he found that all hunters divided their catch equally with the entire group. THANKS were not demanded or even accepted, because that would intimate that the giver was superior or that the receiver would not give something whenever he could.[6]

It was not even a barter system, with an equal gift exchanged. The members of the tribe merely agreed to SHARE whatever they could catch or gather, even with those who had slept all day or made tools. In this manner, everyone was accepted and taken care of, no matter what their expertise. Superiority and inferiority cannot exist in a society where no one can rule.

Without HIERARCHY, each individual takes full responsibility for his actions or lack of actions. Within our complex society, there is a possibility of a HORIZONTAL hierarchy, where each person will have some organizational power due to his abilities but not the power to dominate another. For example, the pilot of a plane has to make sure all are seated for their own safety while he flies the plane, but he is not on a big ego-trip about it.

Each decade seems to have its own flavor and causes. The sixties was a time of re-evaluating roles and ideas with emphasis on the individual. The seventies was a time of dancing and the exposing of extreme political corruption. The eighties showed a return to ancient spiritual beliefs and techniques, balanced by wars and a call for world cooperation.

The 90s will have to develop a GLOBAL CONSCIOUSNESS if it continues in the direction of freedom started in the late eighties. We have outgrown the divided world. All of our decisions must be

---

[6] LIFE WITHOUT CHIEFS, New Age Magazine, Nov/Dec 1989

with recognition of the entire Earth, one large equal TRIBE of equal individuals.

Each of these past decades has seen a general acceptance of common ideas which groups have propounded and fought for. This is a larger GANG, still asking for sacrifice. It is always important to remain an individual if you offer support to any cause. To join any group will limit your ideas and possibly dictate your actions. Be yourself.

FASHION has always acted as a statement of which group or social class you belong to, or a statement of individuality. The fifties looked TOUGH, the sixties looked WILD, the seventies looked COOL, and the eighties brought a revolution in styles as women refused to wear the junk they were offered as fashion.

The youth of today seem to have brought fashion to new extremes. If you love to shave half your head, stick a bone through your nose and wear clashing fluorescent clothing with holes in it; that's fine. Just remember that you might only attract others with the same look. Have fun with it, but know that your looks are not YOU.

The rebel will not wear clothing just because the gang wears it. She will decide what she'll wear. Proclaiming your individuality by dressing like other rebels makes you another sheep. Wear what you LIKE!

Although I am not in favor of gangs, because individuality is lost there, I am not at all against meeting with friends and interacting. A real friend will not IMPOSE anything on you. If people are allowed to grow and change, there may come a time when you are not in tune with old friends. You'll meet new people and there is no reason to force old friendships. Don't make friendship into another bondage.

COMMUNICATION with friends is important, especially to teenagers. You are getting new ideas and new interests and speaking to others about them can help you to understand the changes you are all going through. Telephones have become a major connector of ideas, as any self-loving teenager already knows.

A group of real friends can support or choose not to support each other in whatever they do. Either way, a friend will not prevent the creativity or freedom of his amigos. There is no peer PRESSURE. Everyone is invited to be utterly himself. Organization kills individuality. A rebel cannot compromise his life by being part of a gang.

Be a majority of ONE!

CHAPTER NINETEEN

ALONELINESS

It has been said a million times, "You are born alone, alone you live, and alone you die." It is an inescapable fact. We all know the truth of this statement, but we may respond to it very differently.

People are scared of strangers, despite the fact that we are all strangers no matter how hard we try to be known to each other. We are changing all the time and others are also. Because of fear, people always try to fit into FAMILIAR groups.

Just sit next to someone on a train, bus or plane. Most of the time, the stranger will want to know where you have come from, where you're going, what you do for a living; all kinds of nonsense so he will find something you have in common. Then he can relax. You are familiar.

Try not answering the questions and see how uneasy the asker gets: reading the same magazine twice, looking out the window, acting like he is busy. If you meditatively look in, even while watching another, it makes him even more squirmy.

This is the DOUBLE-EDGED sword spoken of by the mystics. Your consciousness is seeing the other, but is also watching yourself seeing the other. In this way, everyone becomes a mirror and you allow yourself to be reflective without any reactions to the outside at all.

LONELINESS is negative. It is a state of discomfort in missing others. It is a dream. The other is not here, and you are bringing the memory here instead of living this moment. In reality, YOU are not here and that is the problem. The only way to finish with loneliness is to go right through it. See, feel, and taste your ALONENESS. It is the only way existence can be. Aloneness is not loneliness. Instead of missing the other, you are enjoying yourself, your space.

Jealousy is closely linked to loneliness. You use the other as a crutch, someone to lean on. But people are not tools and don't like to be used and possessed. It is amazing that people "fall in love" and wind up only hurting each other. This is not love, it is a subtle slavery.

The only way to break out of possessiveness and jealousy is to face it. My second year of fighting fires, I had just split up with a girl with whom I'd spent over three years. She was writing me letters from all over the states, about her new lovers and what fun places they were going next. Luckily, I had started meditating.

Of course, I was jealous. There was no one fun to be with on forest fires, or was there? There was ME! I learned that every time I was getting exhausted, my mind would run off to imagine where she was and what she was doing. This became my ALARM clock. Whenever I was daydreaming, it made me feel sad and heart-broken. This was my cue to snap myself back to the present moment. Here I was, out in the National Forest with the birds singing, all nature celebrating, and I joined in.

Every day for a month, I would wake up and do a cathartic meditation to release the pain I was feeling and transform it into energy for work. I must have cried, and laughed, for over a month before the pain eased and I felt as light as a feather. It was not only this one girl. The fear of being alone had deep ROOTS in my childhood, and I used this new situation to dig out all the old stuff. This was real house-cleaning.

Learning to be alone is not necessarily a horrible experience. In fact, the only way to see your aloneness is to be very intimate. Two lovers soon find the closest space that they can come to each other, and then it becomes impossible to come closer. They are two and they are trying to be one. There is a BORDER which stops just short of merger, and from there you have to move away again.

This can cause misery if you still insist on the impossible merger, but to a rebel everything is another learning experience. You cannot become PHYSICALLY one with another. It is a fact. You are alone. The deeper you move into aloneness, the more beautiful it becomes.

When aloneness starts helping your inner search, many seekers have to get away from the crowds for a while, to go deeper within, undisturbed. The fever of trying to succeed slowly fades and a cool breeze enters. When aloneness becomes a continuous experience, it is time to return to the marketplace. Only with many others around you, doing all kinds of hilarious things to each other, can you see how deep your meditation has gone.

From that point on, EVERYONE is your mirror. By seeing the magnification of your own traits in others, you can easily understand more about yourself and your fears. Fear drops the day you come in contact with the center, the part that even death cannot take away. It was always there, but you had been looking outward, hoping for security and success.

The only lasting security comes from accepting INSECURITY. If you can really see that life goes on whether you try to change it or not, you can relax and see which way it goes. Then you can go with it. Death will come someday, and then you can relax and see what that is. You've lived life with acceptance and you don't want to miss the grand exit.

World peace starts right here, within. If someone comes home to herself and starts laughing and dancing, others will feel it. It is not an effort. And world peace isn't a thing. It is a huge world covered with interacting individuals, and each will have to come to their individual peace.

I met a Peace Worker who was going to chain herself dramatically to a fence outside a nuclear test site. I asked her if she was at peace within herself or was she full of anger toward the nuclear industry. She said that her own transformation would take too long and that action had to be taken now. In some ways, she could see the point. She was demanding that others should drop their well-paid jobs in the interest of world peace, but she was not interested in her own inner peace.

Within the anti-nuclear group, she was considered a great martyr, ready to go to jail. Many of those protesters were angry, throwing things at the plant, sitting in the road to block them. How can anger bring peace?

To escape from the fact of aloneness, many people join clubs or churches. In an effort to cover the fact of aloneness, the priests have invented God as a father, the great teddy bear in the sky. It is a consolation, but this concept has been used to exploit people through their fear, making the churches the most wealthy institutions on the Earth.

The concept of an exterior God, from which you are separated, keeps you looking outward, begging for help. Prayer shows a

LACK of trust in what existence is offering you, and it keeps you involved, so you never experience the inner silence.

Clubs give the illusion that you are needed, special, and accepted by a group. All kinds of clubs are formed as buffers against the reality of being alone. Even watching the television can be an escape from loneliness. The viewer can become identified with the actors, as if the ACTION is happening to them. Football fans choose a team to become part of their ego and hope they win. All that fighting and effort over a stupid little ball. My partner, Mati, once asked why they don't just give both teams a ball so they can stop arguing.

For married couples who are trying to act like they are one, these same clubs offer refuge from the other half. So many husbands and wives join clubs or go to watch a game, just to get AWAY from their spouses, and to get nurtured by the attention of the crowd. Instead of love, they settle for group ego.

People get mixed up when they hear quotes like, "We are all one." It doesn't mean we have to all ACT like one. Neither does it mean we need to control others.

When a Mystic says this, he is speaking from an experience of going beyond the personality, beyond the individual mind. Without the layers of societal programming and accumulated knowledge, there is one consciousness. But unless it is an EXPERIENCE, it is a LIE.

There is no way to share this experience with the group. Each individual must journey into her own center. Silence and bliss are contagious and others may be affected, whether they know it or not. Anyone in their center invites everyone else to their center without a word spoken.

That is why in India, everyone goes to sit with his spiritual guide at least once a year if possible. It is not for teaching and learning. It is called darshan, sitting quietly with the Awakened One and allowing your center to come on fire. It is communion, not communication. It cannot be taught, it can only be caught.

An enlightened being is like a catalyst, speeding up the process of growth merely by his/her presence. In physics, ENTROPY describes the tendency for unused energy in a closed system to move into chaos. Adding energy back into this system by opening it brings ORDER.

This is exactly the case with human consciousness. By wasting energy in social interaction, thinking and analysis, controlling emotions and natural drives, we fall unconscious. In utter aloneness, the presence of a master sparks the new energy for spiritual experience. It may happen to many individuals, but not to a group. There is no teaching needed, no organization to feel identified with. Then this same openness must be found without the crutch of a master, a direct oneness with the WHOLE.

My experiences with an Enlightened One were scientific, observing the effects of the Master's presence within and in others. Sometimes I'd try not to feel anything, and I might feel more because I was not TRYING to feel it. Effort is a way to block spiritual nature.

From the outside, a spiritual master seems to be surrounded by followers, another gang. Actually, only LIONS, individuals, are attracted to a real master. Just because each has an unknown link to the master's energies, they sit in the same presence, but there is nothing they have in common. Each will flower in her own way, as existence has created her.

I'm sure there are many so-called saints all over the world who are not enlightened and manage to gather FOLLOWERS with trickery. If you are impressed with trickery, then you will be exploited. This SPIRITUAL exploitation can ruin your trust in a guide and keep you from seeking further. It is a crime and most organized religions are guilty of it.

THE SPIRITUAL EGO

There is no possibility of FOLLOWING another. Each one of us has to go within the spiritual realm alone. A real guide will not give orders and will expect no obedience. Always remember, if you follow someone, you will wind up where he was going, instead of where you were going.

Aloneness is the reality. We can share the love and compassion which flow from one center to another, and that makes it an authentic sharing. There is no need to CULTIVATE love, or it will be false. Acting compassionate is so ugly. It reduces the other to a thing, a rung on the ladder to heaven. Don't climb on people.

When love wants to pour through us, we simply allow it. In finding your SELF, you lose the fear of death which will allow others to come close without scaring you. Intimacy can only happen to centered people.

Those who attempt to escape from themselves by leaving the WORLD and living in monasteries are cowardly. They're so afraid of their own thoughts and actions that they run to be alone. This is not true aloneness, it is escaping. Within the confines of the monastery or the mountains, the monk or nun can feel safe and cultivate a religious attitude. But bring that actor back into the market place and all the desires and miseries will rush back in.

There is the story of a man who left his wife and family, his kingdom and his wealth, and walked off into the Himalayas. Many seekers found their way to the mountain where this man was sitting and he became well-known as a spiritual teacher.

Unexpectedly, his wife, who had been searching for years, found him one day and fell at his feet. She was weeping with joy at finding him and showed no anger for his leaving her alone to raise the children. One of the disciples noticed his guru was shaking.

After the wife left, the disciple approached the master. "I saw you quivering with fear before that woman. You are a fake. You have not really left the world, you are still carrying it within. Your wife was totally forgiving and loving. She has transformed herself and is more enlightened than you are."

With that, the disciple jumped to his feet and ran after the guru's wife. The fear of being disturbed had alerted the disciple to his master's hypocrisy. The authentic center can never be disturbed. It is, as John Lily put it, *"The Center of the Cyclone"*. All the insanities of the world are happening, maybe even in your own mind, and you can just watch them go by, like traffic in the street. A time comes when you become your best friend.

I recently received a letter from a Russian teenage girl who said she had no friends in the Soviet Union. I replied that most people have no real friends even though they believe they have many. It amazes me the way people lie and cheat each other for very minor reasons, even those they consider their best friends. The fear seems to be that their friend won't like the truth so it is okay to lie. Then what is friendship?

True friends accepted each other as they are. They may be totally different in looks, ideas and opinions, but they enjoy their differences. Friendship cannot be an attempt to escape from loneliness, but should be a sharing of two whole individuals, a meeting of two worlds. In utter silence, true friends become one. Without the chattering minds, we merge. It takes strength in yourself and guts to allow intimacy, but merging is its own reward.

Accepting your aloneness, you start allowing others freedom to be alone. Only two alone people can really meet, and move away again without the fear that makes lovers grab onto each other and kill the love.

In our aloneness, we are all ONE; but in trying to be part of the group, we are not even OURSELVES.

CHAPTER TWENTY

Creativity can manifest in anything you do. Even a mundane act like washing the dishes can become a creative event. Just feel the warm water on your hands. See how you are transforming dirty dishes into sparkling clean dishes. You may start singing, enjoying the washing.

The trick is in the ability to ENJOY your own energy, in whatever you are doing. A job that used to be toil, becomes playful and fun.

Naturally, it's easier to be around other people who are interested in freedom, creativity and love. Even finding one person who is supportive of you in whatever you wish to try is a real blessing.

Religions have always called God the CREATOR of the world. The new consciousness today indicates that God is the CREATIVITY happening each moment in all existence. If, for even a single moment, the primal energies which hold existence together were cut off, all life would vanish. Life is breathing in you and beating in your heart, whether you are a murderer or a tiny baby. The gift is unconditional.

If you accept that God is creativity, the only way to participate is to CREATE. Plant seeds, paint pictures, make music, let your energies flow into anything life-affirmative and you are in harmony with the universe.

There are two types of creativity. One is only a busy-ness that people do to keep occupied so they never have to face their loneliness and misery. This kind of creativity is seen all over the world. The WORKAHOLICS can't sit still for a moment. They want to feel USEFUL and needed because they haven't discovered the silent spaces within.

The second type of creativity is not an escape from the inner journey, it is a FLOWERING of that journey. When the heart lights up with orgasmic joy, you want to express it. You are too full of love and it is overflowing. Whatever you do out of this creativity will have beauty and will be an invitation to others to DISAPPEAR into the art or music.

When you can enjoy doing whatever it is that you do, you then have the key to contentedness. There is no goal far away that you have to go toward. Life is made of SIMPLE things, and to do them creatively is to love what you do.

Remember the last time you fell in love, maybe this morning? The whole world was transformed. All was bright and beautiful. Nothing could shoot you down and you were prone to singing and dancing.

The only problem with love for another is that it changes. One day it blossoms with such color, you can't imagine it'll ever die. The next day you may be sitting with the dried petals, no life left in the flower.

As I've said, love can become a STATE OF CONSCIOUSNESS which can stay without anyone else being there. When the heart opens to itself, to the entire universe, it can LAST and be shared with all.

Once it gets started, the inventive movement is infectious. People come to visit us while Mati is making sweaters and I am doing beadwork, making puppets or writing. Often, we are asked if there is anything for our guests to play with. One pulled out her tee-shirts and did beautiful paintings on them.

For me, each burst of creativity is followed by a quiet space. It is as if the rain cloud gets full and has to pour. Then it must wait until it is filled again before another shower. Meditation refills the space with energy and it is expressed through some form of art, writing or music.

I've never suffered from the proverbial WRITER'S BLOCK. I try not to get in the way of my own writing. By not thinking about writing with the conscious mind, I can allow the larger, subconscious mind to write. Later, I can work out the mechanics and wording. The ideas flow from the silence and I write them down.

Without effort is the only way to open and let existence create through you and I never even try to write unless it is happening. Most great writers, artists, musicians and dancers have spoken about allowing the creativity to come through them. Some see the painting in dreams, artists vanish into the work for hours, dancers disappear into the dance.

I'm not speaking of channelling. I have found no other beings to speak through me and I don't know if there is such a thing. Most channellers I've encountered seem to have too many commercials. I am speaking of full-brain writing, painting or whatever you are doing, allowing the WHOLE to create through you. The intuition COMPOSES and the intellect RECORDS.

Creativity is a state of participation with the universe and can bring a new quality into everything you do. Clothing and ornamentation present infinite chances to fabricate new fashions. Writing and painting are equally viable means of self-expression, but don't always make your living since they are not always useful or wearable forms of art.

The theater and performing arts can be immensely helpful in your meditations also. Since the actress has to become someone else, but deep inside she knows she is not the character, it gives insight into WATCHING. As Shakespeare noted, "All the world's a stage and all the men and women merely players."

Everything we SHOW to others is an act, in a way, because our reality cannot be given. Knowing that you are acting most of the time frees you to be a creative actor and enjoy the show. Being in a stage or screen production allows you to step into someone else's shoes and get a look at their world. If you can keep that awareness all the time, you need not get identified with your own script.

The amazing thing about pouring your energies into anything is that your energy INCREASES as you get more totally INVOLVED. Your work becomes your growth, without any struggle, you allow yourself to become the project. A creative HIGH is not hazardous to your body and is not illegal; but it is sure to become habit-forming and infectious!

Art reflects the consciousness of the artist. We have just come through a time of pain and hopelessness as the world has been teetering on the brink of disaster for decades. The art has been cathartic and violent. It may have been therapeutic for Picasso to paint nightmares, but it's ugly to me. Now we are seeing the first examples of a new art, an art of beauty and peace.

Nature is constantly moving toward balance. Whenever life moves to one extreme, it gets pulled toward the opposite to balance. When there is war, a vast amount of creative energy is available simultaneously. I, personally, spent the first few days of the Persian Gulf War creating and writing. It wasn't that I needed to keep busy because I was nervous, but because a wave of creativity swept me into action. When you get the hang of it, you can bring a new dimension into everything you are a part of. New ideas come pouring into the quiet space you have found within. Even sitting quietly and doing nothing, the creative energies BURN like a candle, lighting your inner world. This is the ultimate creativity and you are doing nothing! That which gets USED in the world can never be as pure as that which remains virgin, unused. Meditation leads you to the source of your own evolution, beyond all effort and struggle. Your own fruition is the highest form of creating. The most daring artist is the one who creates HERSELF!

CHAPTER TWENTY-ONE

NATURE PROOF

All through this book, I have been telling you about NATURAL living as the way to blissfulness. "But where is the proof?" you ask. "Who in this world lives naturally?"

There is a tribe in Baster, India, known as the Hill Marias. Their living conditions are primitive and natural. They live in caves and bamboo huts, have few material possessions, and have no concept of private ownership of land. So far, the arriving missionaries have not upset their way of life.

These are the people I mentioned earlier who have no condemnation of sex. As soon as children are old enough to be interested in sex, they move to a communal house in the center of the village, called the GHOTUL. Here, they are allowed to have sexual relations with all the members of the opposite sex. The only rule is that they should not remain with the SAME partner for more than three nights.

In this way, every youth becomes familiar with every possible partner in the village before choosing to be married. There is nobody who feels inferior because all get plenty of love and affection. When a couple chooses to be married, they both know that this is the best choice and divorce is virtually unheard of. The society makes the couple wait up to two years before the marriage even after the decision is made.

Unrepressed sexuality in this manner teaches nonpossessiveness. Sexual drives are natural and accepted. Seriousness and jealousy are erased and sex becomes a light-hearted play. The people, 13,500 of them, live almost naked and no man is interested in a woman's breasts. Breasts are for children. Only the newly-arrived missionaries are interested in breasts. That which is tabooed becomes obsessive.

But what effect does natural living have on these tribal people? Among the Hill Marias, suicide is completely unknown and only one murder is recorded, in which the killer walked 200 miles through the jungle to turn himself in to authorities. The people are innocent and honest. Interestingly, there is no homosexuality or masturbation.

The tribal members are very generous, not hoarding possessions. Each year, on a special occasion they give all their accumulated wealth as gifts to others in a sort of redistribution of wealth. The Hill Marias don't know how to read or write, have no mathematics, have no concept of history or geography, but they are extremely happy. They know how to dance, sing, and love each other.

One of the most interesting aspects of this UNREPRESSED culture is that the people are reported rarely to have dreams. Psychologists say that dreams are often caused by unfinished business from the daytime. Dreams satisfy the yearning to do something which was not completed, such as meeting a person you can't actually meet because of social morals.

By not repressing anything during the waking hours, there is nothing for the Hill Marias to finish in the dream state. Mostly, they report dreamless sleep, which is known in India as SUSHUPTI.

Enlightened people of all cultures have reported Sushupti, the end of dreams, as a forerunner to their enlightenment. When the mind is cleansed of all the repressions, and the meditative watcher becomes strong, there is no need to purge pent up garbage through dreaming.

Because of the rarity of dreams, the Hill Marias consider the few dreams they have as a reality. If they hurt or insult another in the dream state, they will take a gift to apologize for the injury, as if it really happened. In this way, they are extremely respectful of each other and take responsibility even for THINKING nasty thoughts.

The Hill Marias population has remained relatively stable since the 1930s while the rest of India suffers from gross overpopulation and poverty. In some manner, natural living has saved them from the extreme poverty and overpopulation of the repressed cultures. There are no priests telling them to make more church members or politicians wanting more soldiers. I have found no information on their birth control methods.

It is said that these simple people have no ENLIGHTENED people, nobody special. If everyone lives naturally, they move into their own awakening without meditation and therapies needed to drop hang-ups. When all tribal members flower as individuals, none stand out. Who notices?

In 1985, the first missionaries were allowed to build a hospital, retail shops, a vocational training center and a school within the Hill Marias region. Colorful saris are influencing girls to cover their breasts and education is beginning.

It appears that the organized religions will destroy one of the few remaining natural villages in the modern world. If so, it will probably be out of jealousy. One question I wish to pose: "Is it better to be illiterate, natural, generous and happy; or is it better to work, read, become MORAL and then need churches to preach afterlife philosophies and psychiatry to deal with your newly-found misery?"

An old African native was being pressured by a Christian missionary to convert. "If you want to get to heaven, you'll have to live by the commandments," he told the chief.

"That mean no sex without marriage? No kill enemies? No steal from other tribes?" the old man asked.

"Wonderful," replied the missionary. "You are getting civilized!"

"No sweat," says the native. "Christian and OLD MAN mean same thing!"

PROGRESS?

CHAPTER TWENTY-TWO

GROWING UP
OR GROWING OLD

Growing up and growing old are two different phenomena. In the sixties, the youth used to warn, "Never trust anyone over thirty." They recognized that thirty was the median age where seriousness takes over and people begin to worry about death. Many settle into careers to feel stable and secure, gathering as much money as they can accumulate and may begin to think about having children.

Why do people of this age suddenly want children? There is a recognition of mortality and a drive to become immortal. Children represent the continuation of life, as if a part of the parent is carried on in the child.

Growing old is really then a mind set, based in fear. There are even teenagers who get old before their time and there are also seventy-year-old mischiefs who are as alive and full of laughter and dance as most children. It is a matter of mind, not age.

The main difference between young and old is the direction of their dreaming. Youth dreams of the future, the whole life is ahead and opportunities abound. Aged people dream of the past, there is no future left, they have already lived and the only way to look is back.

Dreams are dreams, they keep you involved in fantasy instead of living here and now. The option overlooked is to stop dreaming altogether and this is the choice of those who grow up instead of old.

What is the mysterious trait called MATURITY, which seems to pop up every time an adult speaks to a teenager? Does it just mean growing serious, or is there a maturity possible for fun-loving rebels also?

To me, SERIOUSNESS is a disease. It means losing the fun and joys of living. The serious person makes everything into work. Even playing has to become a GAME where there is a winner, hopefully himself. The serious man will not participate in anything which doesn't offer him a chance for glory. If he is unable to participate in a game, he will watch others, maybe on the television. If his team wins, he has won. If not, he is defeated. It is a very serious affair.

The CREATIVE REBEL cannot get stuck in seriousness. There is too much fun in life to waste it on struggles for power and recognition. The creative person will make even his work into play. He is SINCERE and will do his best, but he cannot get serious and angry if he fails.

By the old definition, maturity seemed to mean taking on burdens and doing your DUTY. All were expected to live up to certain criteria to prove their value, and then they would be accepted as mature individuals. It was a reward for accepting domination.

Maturity, in my definition, means bringing yourself totally into each situation, being absolutely INVOLVED. A mature person takes responsibility for everything he does, and even what he doesn't do, but could have done. Each action must be decided by his own intelligence and experience. No mature person can carry out an order if it goes against his heart.

An immature person is worried about what others think about him. He will do almost anything to be "one of the group". In this way, the GROUP becomes the master, and he becomes the slave, allowing others to use him in exchange for their pseudo-friendship.

For young adults, who seem to crave acceptance, it is easy to be swayed by peer pressure. A mature person cannot be dared into doing stupid things like drugs, theft, dangerous stunts, or anything else which he knows is unloving or unintelligent. A mature individual will hang out with mature friends or he will be alone. No one can force him into betraying his intelligence.

In our attempts to meet each other and drop our hang-ups, we can often misunderstand each other. Arguing is usually a result of misunderstood ideas. To be mature in communications, we must accept that we will sometimes misinterpret others and they may not understand us.

Anger can flare up to defend our ideas, but that will only cause wounds. If we can see that each moment is NEW and the people around us are changing as we are, then there is never any reason to carry a grudge. Be alone until your anger has passed. When you meet again, remember never to go back to discuss the argument. Two new people are meeting now.

The rebel has no ENEMIES. Holding a grudge is using someone else as a scapegoat for problems you haven't worked out in yourself. This doesn't mean that you have to MAKE friends with everyone either. Some people absolutely SUCK your energy with intellectual babble and there is nothing wrong with avoiding these parasites, but they are not enemies.

If you wish to share with others, see who is the most nurturing to you and open for you to nurture them. This doesn't mean you have to act goody-goody either. People who are grounded and creative allow you to be absolutely authentic in their presence. Mature people INSPIRE each other.

Communication is a BASE form of meeting. Two people who are afraid of each other have to talk because it is the only bridge between them. It takes extreme courage to sit in absolute silence with a stranger, looking into each other's eyes. Both may feel too vulnerable, as if their entire beings are exposed.

COMMUNION is a more refined meeting and can only happen in silence, on an energy level. To allow communion between two beings, or between one being and the entire existence, needs strength and maturity. It is as if a fruit has ripened; no one can make it ripen, but it comes naturally with time.

Many who've become enlightened have never spoken again, but may only sing or play music as a form of sharing. Hotei, the best-loved saint in Japan, was known as the LAUGHING BUDDHA. He would walk from town to town and stand in the center of the market place, laughing. Soon, his joy would become contagious and the whole town would roar with laughter.

This is the power of the Awakened Ones. They are not interested in domination or being worshipped, but only in sharing the immense joy they've found. In a way, they are more fragile than other people because most of their energies are involved in their spirits, not in their bodies; but their gifts affect everyone they meet.

Life comes in WAVES. The best time to go outward is when the energy is up and creativity is at a peak. When you are off, and a bit tired, it is time to rest. Go inside, relax, and wait for the energies to rise again. Maturity calls for an understanding of life cycles. Instead of being caught in the ups and downs, the rebel knows change will always come and remains flexible.

The mature rebel overcomes the FEVERISH attitudes of youth but never loses the clarity of vision and mischievous joys of youth. There is no rush to accumulate knowledge, possessions, or friends. All these things are desired by people who know something is missing in their lives and are trying to find it OUTSIDE in the world.

The real jewels are hidden WITHIN. By reconnecting to the sources of life within you, the fever subsides into a cool, calm LET GO. Only then can the seeker's life become trusting. Deep relaxation is a side-effect of total acceptance.

Hero worship appears to be on the decline, and rightfully so. Heroes have always been used by the society as role models, which keeps the worshipper feeling inferior. Everyone should be his own hero. Sports figures made good heroes because they had to sacrifice much for the team. A fan wishing to follow their hero's example would understand that sacrifice is the way to be accepted. Societies love to sacrifice individuals to causes.

Many movie stars find that FAME is more of a curse than a blessing once they succeed in gathering fans. Wherever they go, they are hounded by fans or journalists who want to know everything about their lives. Deep inside, they know that it is the ACT which has attracted these people, not who they really are. Their private life is no longer private.

Scandal magazines expose the faults of famous people to anxious readers. But why are readers interested in slanderous gossip? It is because they are JEALOUS of the fame. By worshipping a famous person or star, the fan feels inferior. His ego is hurt because he would like all the attention that the star gets. It is hard to forgive someone who makes you feel inferior. You would rather see them fail so you can feel superior. This is IMMATURITY.

Most people measure their status by their accomplishments. Whatever they do becomes part of the ego. A person who doesn't know himself will become identified with his job, getting recognition from the society or company for his "good work". He needs to feel useful before he can accept himself.

Without acceptance, it is easy to get caught in self-destructive activities. A person who feels unworthy also feels angry. To one extent or another, most of us have been taught to feel unworthy of life's gifts.

Have you seen what happens when someone RETIRES? Many go into depression, feeling that they are not needed anymore. I've witnessed perfectly healthy people get sick and die right after retirement. The meaninglessness of life catches up when the usefulness ceases.

Seeing this, you can choose another way to live your life: in CREATIVE REBELLION. Don't be concerned with the judgments of others. Are they happy? Has their choice to work for acceptance really paid off?

The focus now becomes YOUR OWN flowering. Since it's almost impossible to make anyone else happy with your actions, and it is absolutely impossible to make everyone accept you, move in the direction where you will be the most contented. You are the only person you have to live up to.

If you are already getting old as a teenager, you can choose to grow young again. One beautiful method comes from the Sufi Master, Jabbar, who lived centuries ago. His technique has been named GIBBERISH. Just sit along or with a group for a half hour and spout nonsense, talk in every language you don't know. Express your emotions and insanity without mind interfering with words and thoughts. Afterward, sit silently.

None of the techniques in this book are miracles which will guarantee a change in your life. It is up to you, how intensely you try these methods. Remember that your outside and inside reflect opposites. If you always smile and think yourself a NICE person, your inside will be serious and egoistic, judgmental and angry. By acting out your frustrations, letting insanity play itself out, your inside gets lighter, more centered and aware.

Instead of getting caught in guilt and self-denial, it is better to see that life SHOWERS gifts on you whether you deserve them or not. Seeing the unconditional love existence pours over us brings gratitude, not guilt.

Look at people who've never allowed themselves to be young and natural. Even in their old age, they still haven't satisfied their sexual drives, or realized the futility of gathering possessions. The "dirty old man" is still obsessed with women's breasts, which should have disappeared in early childhood.

Grow up with humor, become alive again and fun will return to your life. With awareness, every tiny ordinary thing becomes deeply satisfying. Laughter comes easily when there is nothing missing and nowhere else to go. Wherever you are is the only goal of this moment. A person who lives life with totality will become more beautiful with age instead of more demanding, fearful and serious.

IMPORTANT NOTICE: Isn't it amazing how bold type draws your attention?

Do you have the courage to be authentically yourself in every situation? The rebel cannot put on a mask for different people to impress them or to gain approval. When you have totally accepted yourself, you can throw away the masks and bring fun to every interaction.

Maturity enables you to understand when you are young, that your health in later life depends on the love you feed your body now. Most teens think they are invincible and push their bodies into a quick old age. We are extremely fragile, but the vigor of youth can deceive us.

By removing the stresses of the modern serious working world, your CELEBRATION keeps you young. There is never any reason to get spiritually senile. Creativity can last until the final breath. Remaining young at heart while sharpening intelligence is a sure sign of maturity.

Existence has created each of us as an absolutely unique individual. Instead of groveling for acceptance, have the guts to be yourself. Maturity takes time and experience, but a right start is needed. Play without competition, laugh for no reason at all, chill out and enjoy being alive.

Grow UP, but never grow OLD.

CHAPTER TWENTY-THREE

THE 90s: THE AGE OF SHARING

How do I view the decade of the 1990s? It is a whole new chance to recreate our world. With the political events of the late eighties still unfolding with such surprise and speed, the nineties are our last chance to sink or swim, or maybe just float and enjoy.

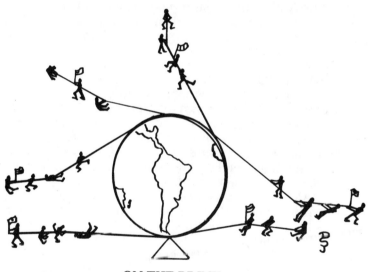

ON THE BRINK

The breakdown of Totalitailanism and Fascism are disrupting all our ideas about who is an enemy and whom we should fear. With expected setbacks, the Soviet block countries are opening within the vision of Mikhail Gorbachev. We have seen the failure of forced Communism, as it appeared in Russia, and we see a reuniting Germany.

Real Communism was supposed to be a SHARING of wealth, which was impossible in an undeveloped country like Russia. It seems that Capitalism is the only system that knows how to produce wealth. After a country is wealthy, wealth can be shared. Our country is in a position to find ways to share our wealth and our methods of gaining wealth with the rest of the world. So far, we haven't even learned to share it with our own countrymen and greed is forcing our economy to its knees.

Communal experimentation is now in progress in Australia and may be an alternative to certain groups of Americans. A voluntary sharing has an entirely different feeling to it than a forced sharing.

Greed has roots in POVERTY. Imagine if everything you need is provided, why would you hoard possessions? Old habits are hard to break. We see even multi-billionaires hoarding their money as if they need it to survive.

Outer wealth is beneficial for relaxing into inner wealth. Only when there is enough food on the table can a man realize that something is still missing, his own spirituality. Those who've lived the American dream and have a house and car and spouse, can see that these things can't make them happy. After each possession is acquired, it is forgotten.

Desire keeps us engaged, so we never have to look into the frightening depths of our beings. It takes great intelligence to see that the pursuit of possessions is more gratifying than the possession itself. Once you own something, it is finished.

Shared wealth gives space to meditate, to finish with the past and to find your true being. A real commune makes sure everybody has his needs fulfilled and shares luxuries. It need not be forced. It should be the choice of the participants, finding whatever it is they would like to create out of abundance, not out of need.

HIERARCHY is not necessary. A gathering of REBELS will not give each other orders. The more people who live together, the more order is needed, but it need not be a domination. Someone is in charge of the train system. He decides when the trains come and go. Someone is responsible for cooking and he decides when the meals will be ready.

As long as the focus of sharing is on allowing the growth of everyone, there will not be domination. Experiments in the sixties with communes proved that you can't accept everyone into a shared environment and expect it'll work out. A prerequisite must be that each member has come to find his own truth and, out of his seeking, chooses to live with others who are also seeking.

CRIME will disappear if we learn to share wealth and stop forcing ourselves into outdated moralities. Individuals who live their lives naturally will never get obsessed with sex and violence. Sexual energies move naturally into LOVE if awareness is present. The same energies move again into the spirit when love is allowed its natural progression. The 90s may see the end of forced beliefs which have led to most of the world's neuroses.

How will we solve the problems with world HUNGER? There is only one way to alleviate this problem, and that is to stop crowding the surface of our planet with more people. BIRTH CONTROL is a must! Our Earth is finite in its ability to support people. If birth control methods had been used for the last thirty years, we would be living in the Garden of Eden again.

ABORTION is a personal matter. If proper birth control methods are used, abortion should not be an issue. Since all religions speak of some form of afterlife or reincarnation, it seems incongruous that they should oppose birth control. If death is an ILLUSION and life is eternal, it is merely a change of form and a postponement of entry into an overcrowded world.

Religions and politicians stand against birth control and abortion for other reasons. Their whole purpose is to make more converts and voters. Politics entered into religion thousands of years ago. Whoever had the most people would rule the nation. Whichever religion had the biggest armies would conquer the non-believers.

We've seen what effects religious programming can have on large groups of people in Iran and Iraq, Ireland and Israel, India and Lebanon. Just put someone in an army and tell him he will go to paradise if he dies in combat against a chosen enemy and hell descends on the Earth.

India was divided by feuding religious fanatics. Despite the division, thousands of Hindus were murdered by Mohammedans and vice versa. Now Sikhs are demanding their own land and want India split again. War and religious ideologies are interconnected.

We need not go so far from home to see religions praising war. Hitler was blessed by the Christian churches in Germany. Just recently, the pre-sent Pope declared in Italy, "To serve the army is a very respectable, beautiful, gentle thing." More people have been murdered over the last two thousand years in the name of CHRISTIAN LOVE than for any other cause.

I feel that the 90s will be our last chance to drop the insanities of the past and to look into true religious EXPERIENCE, instead of religious DOCTRINE. While science explores the outside world, meditation is the science of the inner world. Without any preconceived ideas, we have to explore the reality of our being. No religious teachings are needed, only guidance as to the methods of exploring.

SCIENCE will need to undergo a turn-around in the 90s. In the past, it has been destructive, dissecting everything. The splitting of the atom was the ultimate in destruction, unleashing a force capable of destroying the entire planet. Dissection cannot offer the secrets of nature. Taking apart a beautiful flower will not reveal the source of the beauty. Looking in the soil will not show you how a plant gets so bright and alive. Discovering beauty takes receptiveness, a FEMININE approach to science.

Traditionally, science has begun with an hypothesis before experimenting. The scientist may conduct his experiment in a certain way to prove the hypothesis. Quantum physics has shown that the experimenter can INFLUENCE the outcome of his experiment by his beliefs. Science must then begin with no preconceived ideas, and strive to find the truth.

Life is very fragile and needs a delicate balance in which to survive. The overpopulation of man has thrown the balance off in every way. The added loss of so many species of birds, animals and plants has changed everything, and it is only the beginning of our own doom.

The CREATIVE REBEL who chooses science will be interested in creation instead of destruction. How does nature create life? How can we improve the quality of life on our ailing planet? How do we make it a better place to live?

In the past, scientists have been forced to work for MILITARY purposes if they wanted government funding. Even our biggest breakthroughs in medicine have been by-products of weapons technologies. A radical shift in funding and priorities can promote the solutions to most of our environmental problems including the ozone layer and rain forest destruction.

Science has the capabilities to SOLVE world hunger and poverty through birth control, ecological healing, better medicines and food sources. Then there is no need to cut the rain forests for temporary jobs. Pollution can be eliminated if all the geniuses of our times focus on the solutions.

The world of the 90s will be decisive. There is no turning back if another world war starts and there is a point where nature has been so disturbed that it cannot rejuvenate itself. The oil disasters of the Persian Gulf War continue to hurt the environment even now. All the insanity of the past seems to have evolved a desire for death, as if life is not worth living.

It used to be almost a sacred ritual that a father would present his son with a gun. Why can't he offer a FLUTE? With all the glorified war movies and television shows, children are taught that killing is something to make you proud. Medals are given for the greatest number of murders in war.

If mankind remains stuck in the bondage of hierarchical structures with fixed belief systems, it is a choice for DEATH. The new world can only be realized through a radical change from beliefs to experience, from nations and separated organizations into a global community and from controlling life to natural living. It is only because there is no joy in most peoples' lives that death is the choice. Don't put off what you really want to do until you finish what you SHOULD do. The day will never come when the shoulds stop. You will die unfulfilled.

People have to start LIVING totally. When death comes, it is better to see that you have tried everything you yearned to do and now you can relax and see where death leads, if it goes anywhere. Bring awareness into every experience of life and you can enjoy a conscious death.

Through meditation, you can discover the part of us that survives death. Then you'll know death is fictional. It is only a change of form. Without the overpowering fear of death, you can be here and enjoy life. Here is where you are, and it's the only place you can be. When death comes, you can enter it alertly.

The ancients in India called the world MAYA, an illusion. It is not that the world is illusory, but how we see it that is false. Looking with prejudice keeps us from seeing what is really there. With our minds wandering off into dreams of the future or past, we miss the present. By dropping KNOWLEDGE, we can explore everything as if for the first time, every time we encounter it.

As the youth of today, you will have a lot to say about the survival of our planet. You'll be choosing the priorities, electing the form of government, healing the ecology. What kind of a world do you want to live in, and leave to future people and animals?

I am not advocating HOPE for the 90s. In a subtle way, hope is another pacifier, keeping us locked into the future. The focus must be in living our lives totally and consciously NOW, and the future will be born out of our joy. Hope also throws the responsibility on others; you pray for peace to happen. The way we live NOW will direct the evolution of the future.

As parents of future children, you can break the unconscious patterns of child raising that have made the world such a mess. Each child is a FELLOW TRAVELLER not a possession. Children need not be talked down to, they are equal human beings. They are intelligent, only lacking in experience. Can you let them explore the world for themselves and grow naturally into whatever they want to do? Can you give UNCONDITIONAL love to them, just because they are alive?

How will you handle the ENVIRONMENTAL problems? In the past, the accepted attitude toward nature has been one of fear and the need to conquer it. In primitive times, the dangers were real and fear was needed. Animals could strike, cold and heat could kill, untold dangers lurked everywhere.

Man has created many environments which make his life easier, and protect him from natural dangers, but many of those cause pollution and damage to the ecosystem. Mankind has lost the CONNECTION to nature which has provided the perfect environment for all life on this planet. Exploitation of our natural resources has been tolerated as long as it has created more jobs.

OOPS!

Now the times have changed. Nature can not be seen as an enemy. It is giving you life this very minute. Nature is at the MERCY of man. Without the recognition that we are not separate from nature, we are doomed to destroy ourselves. Nature has a tremendous ability to create harmony, and also to destroy. We are stirring the kettle, making worse storms and changing weather patterns with our pollution.

Whatever you decide to do, bring AWARENESS into it. Whenever we learn anything, we program it into the memory, the robot part of the brain. It becomes reactionary. To bring awareness back, we will have to deprogram the robot and do everything spontaneously and with intelligence. Make every moment new.

For a while, we may make mistakes again because the conscious part of the mind is not used to doing mundane actions. Soon, everything will settle and take on a new creativity because each moment will be a fresh chance to participate with your whole being. When you are totally involved, every doing becomes a meditation, an act of awareness. Then your actions will reflect the flowering of your consciousness.

If you tune into the beauty within there is no reason to be a missionary. You can't give your experience to anyone else; others will also have to wade through layers of personality and conditioning to find themselves. Why get persecuted by those who are afraid to hear anything new?

There is no need to SPEAK about your inside discoveries at all, unless someone asks and wants advice. To step out in front of the congregation and point out their hypocrisies will only get you a mob of enemies. You may wind up like Salmon Rushdie, never able to show his face in public again, even for writing pure fiction.

No one with a lifetime of INVESTMENT in beliefs wants to hear truth. Every enlightened person has been persecuted for bringing in doubts. Al-Hillaj Mansoor was beheaded, Jesus was crucified, Buddha was stoned, Socrates was poisoned, and recently, my spiritual friend, Osho was forced out of the United States and died of apparent poisoning. The only crime of all these men was that they STEPPED OUT of the accepted beliefs and declared their freedom from the past traditions.

If you find your silent space within, enjoy it. It will be felt by others in your presence. All of us have a creative potential which needs energy from the center, only we are unaware of it. The awareness of it does not make you special or superior, you become absolutely content to be ordinary.

CLEAR your vision by dropping ideas and prejudices and see life as it is. Any choice will be only half, life is made up of both sides of everything. Instead of making a choice and going to one extreme or the other, remain in the middle. Gautam Buddha called his path to enlightenment the middle path; remain centered.

Instead of only working at an acceptable level as most workers do, probably around 10% of their potential, the CREATIVE REBEL pours herself into everything she does. The more energy she gives to creativity, the more energy life showers on her.

History reveals only the names of insane people and the statistics of crimes they've committed against humanity. The past has been filled with violence and war. These are not the tools of the Creative Rebel. In breaking with the ways of the past, our future will be filled with love and compassion, creativity and freedom.

Everyone dreams of a better life, without wars and terrorists, without poverty and pollution. It is ONE world and the separations of nations, political groups and religions will have to dissolve back into one harmonious humanity. The spiritual transformation of today's youth can make this world a healthy and loving place to be passed on to future generations.

There is no need to DESTROY the old world, only to CREATE the new one. Others will see the benefits of the new ways and a transformation will happen naturally, with no leaders or followers. I wish to announce the beginning of **THE AGE OF SHARING!**

TEACHING can be merely a method of conditioning the mind, trying to convince others to believe in your point of view. Teachers are above those whom they teach. Education, as such, places knowledge on a pedestal, as if knowing ABOUT life is enough.

SHARING has a totally different vibe to it. All are equal and everyone has something unique to offer. A rebel may help many people, but only by being himself. He cannot look down to anybody, not even a small child. Experiences make each being a new phenomenon and sharing may create a thirst in others to search in a similar manner. Still, no one is a savior and no one is a sinner.

The CREATIVE REBEL will allow love to grow, but he does not feel superior because he is growing. There is nothing more ugly than a spiritual ego. History has been cursed with holier-than-thou do-gooders, out to save the world. Missionaries HUMILIATE those they claim to be helping, often purchasing converts with food and clothing.

There will always be people who'll be jealous of your bliss and will wish to drag you back into the misery of the masses. If you LAUGH too much in a serious world, you are thought to be crazy. Until your heart is strong enough to withstand hatred, it is best to keep your spiritual experiences a secret.

Being a REBEL is not enough. Few rebels of the past have created anything beautiful in this world. CREATIVITY is also not enough. Without an intelligent break from past traditions and conditionings, we are doomed to a world of separation, poverty, hatred and wars.

Only the CREATIVE REBEL can instigate the radical changes which can free our world from seriousness and death-orientation. Only individuals can take the jump inward to true spiritual experience, transforming all their actions into statements of love and freedom.

Whether it is in music, art, dance, science, building or any menial job, the CREATIVE REBEL will bring beauty to whatever she does. Clearing techniques and meditation bring her beyond catharsis, beyond intellect, and into harmony with the universal life forces. Her very being, her presence invites others to celebrate life and to drop out of the serious conditionings which have ruled the past. She does not TRY to guide others, they must join out of their own freedom. Just seeing the integrity and joy of the Creative Rebel, others become inspired to find their own unique contributions to existence. Looking at each situation with a creative eye, new and better ways are discovered. One day I was in a pizza chain store and I saw the way they deliver and package carry-out pizzas in a huge cardboard box which is then discarded. What a WASTE! How many trees must be cut down daily to serve pizzas? I decided to figure out a better way.

That night, I composed a letter to the pizza chain, suggesting they should come up with a REUSABLE plastic box. The customer would pay for the packaging only on their first order. Every order after that, they could get credit for returning one of the reusable boxes which would then be sterilized. The pizza would cost less without the cardboard boxes, the trees would be saved, and the pizza chain could advertise how they were saving the environment.

Now I wait to see if they decide to try my plan. If they ignore me, I'll seek help from the media and we can all force them to comply. If all of us look at new ways to handle all situations dealing with environment and health, we'll make it through the coming crisis ... together!

It seems that whenever something goes to one extreme, it has to go to the opposite extreme to balance. The USSR has been in total domination for so long and now we see freedom reforms sweeping the European globe. Here in the USA, we've enjoyed living in a much freer state, and we now see the government trying to gain more controls.

This is called the PENDULUM theory: one extreme, then the opposite. It is a natural consequence of human effort. The insight of the mystics says that there is a state beyond dualities, when the pendulum stops, right in the center. Buddha called it the *Middle Road,* Taoists call it the *Watercourse Way,* Zen people call it *Finding Your Original Face* and I call it *Nowness.*

There have only been two periods of history: WAR and PREPARATION FOR WAR. PEACE has never happened, because true peace can only come to individuals, not to masses. Miserable people need excitement to break out of their boredom and war supplies plenty of excitement. One madman like Iraq's Hussein and all the armies of the world are ready to fight.

Don't focus on WORLD PEACE or you'll miss your own peace. If you discover the light and bliss of your own center, it will be contagious, but will not need effort. Laughter, dancing and celebration can heal the old world of its terminal seriousness. CREATIVE REBELLION is not a thing, but a PROCESS. Instead of trying to become something; like a doctor, lawyer, American, Russian, black, white, man, woman or any other label, the Creative Rebel enjoys being a process of GROWTH and change, although his interior consciousness remains centered in the present moment. Our world needs a good scrubbing, a cleansing of all past insanities and we need VOLUNTEERS.

Sometimes it's good to know when to JUST SAY YES!

YES!

THE HEART

(APPENDIXES ARE USELESS)

I was lucky enough to be raised by two agnostics who never forced any belief systems on me, leaving me free to investigate and decide for myself where I wanted to look. From my earliest childhood, I was a scientist, needing proof for every spiritual belief offered.

My classmates often asked me, "Don't you love Jesus?" I had never met the guy. They were afraid I was going to burn in hell, but I told them, "If you help a poor man on the street because you want to go to heaven, you're greedy. If I help the same man, it's because I feel for him. I don't know if there's a heaven."

Following my period as a healer and rainmaker, I headed down the road with only a pack on my back, asking existence to lead me beyond my ego-trips to something REAL. I hit California, went up to Washington and into Montana. There, I saw the mountains I had visited in my dreams of being a Blackfeet Indian.

That same day, I was handed a book by the man who would eventually become my spiritual guide and friend, the Indian Mystic, Osho. Here was a true REBEL. I read two paragraphs before I realized I had found someone who was a living embodiment of ENLIGHTENMENT.

He was explaining the difference between POWER, pitting your will against some reality you don't like, and MEDITATION, transforming yourself so you can accept all that life offers. There was no teaching, dogmas or disciplines, only a need to grow in awareness.

I completely dropped my healings and rainmaking and spent over ten years coming close to Osho and going out on my own, getting a taste of my highest potential, and seeing if I could keep it out in the world. I don't want to offer many details of my disciplehood because I don't want to fill your heads with more INFORMATION. This was the way I found myself. You have to find your own way.

My own experiences are beyond words and no one can give their experiences to another. I speak to you about OSHO simply to show that there are people on this Earth who are not stuck in the ruts we create for ourselves. Don't think I'm trying to sell you a PATH. Any teaching, any path will lead you AWAY from yourself.

Instead of explaining all the workshops, the blissful moments of emptiness and the love which still beats in my heart, I try to bring the qualities of NO MIND to my **TEENWORK WORKSHOPS** so teens can have a taste of their own interiority without a bunch of intellectual jabber. I am not an enlightened master, just a fellow traveller with some insights to share.

The quest to find yourself begins by unloading all the baggage, grows through meditative watching, and flowers when you drop all separations and merge back into the whole. It shouldn't be rushed or forced. Be a scientist. Doubt everything! When you find that which is beyond doubt, you've discovered TRUTH.

When you are young, it is natural to fall in love many times, to be sexual, to get drunk once in a while, to climb many mountains and sail many seas. As you get older, sex naturally loses much importance and love takes its place. Even later, love internalizes and creativity becomes of prime importance. This is where I am now.

Although I've had many tastes of ENLIGHTENMENT, TELEPATHY and NO MIND, it has not yet become my norm and I see no need to push. As the Zen Master Basho once said, "Sitting silently, doing nothing, the spring comes and the grass grows by itself."

If you are interested in TEENWORK WORKSHOPS write to:

TeenworK™

c/o MYSTIC GARDEN PRESS
BOX 51, CRESTONE, CO 81131
Tel (719) 256-4137

INDEX

Send copies of

to your favorite teenagers!

Write to:
Mystic Garden Press
BOX 51, CRESTONE, CO 81131
or call:
(719) 256-4137 • VISA/MC accepted

------------------------------------✂------------------------
Please send me _____ copies of
**CREATIVE REBELLION: Positive Options
For Teens In The 90s**
Enclosed is a check, money order or VISA/MC information
for $11.95 plus $1.50 postage and handling per copy.
VISA/MC # _____exp date_____
Signature_____

_____
name
_____
address
_____
city, state, zip

also by **Daniel S. Johnson**

Just released as a German translation!

YHANTISHOR
A FANTASY BASED IN TRUTH

------------------------------------✂------------------

Please send me _____ copies of
YHANTISHOR:
A FANTASY BASED IN TRUTH
Enclosed is a check, money order or VISA/MC information
for $12.95 plus $1.50 postage and handling per copy.
VISA/MC # _____exp date_____
Signature_____

TO:_____
name

_____
address

_____
city, state, zip

"The sort of novel that can change lives!"
-The Book Reader